PCKLED

Freddie Janssen

Over 60 inspiring recipes for pickles, kimchi, vinegars & more

Photography by Helen Cathcart
Illustrations by Melina Bucholz

hardie grant books

Contents

Why Pickling?

This is a question I get asked all the time. Often, I will get a bit flustered and go on a long rant about how I started making pickles and kimchi a few years ago for pop-ups and supper clubs, and how I just can't get enough of the tangy flavours.

There's also the fact that I grew up in Holland. Friday nights were when my mum, sister and I would get a takeaway of proper Dutch fries with mayonnaise, and either a *frikandel speciaal* (a fried sausage smothered in curry sauce, mayonnaise and chopped raw white onions) or a *satekroket* (a croquette with a peanutty satay sauce filling). Without fail I would order an Amsterdam onion from the huge glass jars that sit on the countertop. The saffron yellow, sweet-and-sour onions were the best things in the world to me – so much so I've included my own take on how to eat these little pickled balls of goodness on page 91. I also have memories of my mum and I snacking on huge, juicy dill gherkins in German beer bars – total goodness. My dad's specialty dish was something he called *Hussel A La Papa*, which literally translates as 'Mix It Up Like Dad', and consisted of leftover fried potatoes, gherkins, pickled onions and a fried egg on top. For breakfast, my sister and I would often slather Heinz Sandwich Spread (a creamy version of piccalilli) on white bread; though, my absolute favourite dish was my mum's version of a *choucroute royale* (sauerkraut with mashed potato, served with sausages, bacon, black pudding and baked apple), and is still something I always look forward to eating when I go back home.

At 17 years old, I had my first job as a waitress at a small Indonesian restaurant where I was introduced to Dutch-Asian pickles, called *atjar* (see page 47) – beautiful, crunchy, sweet and sour pickles that were served alongside *rijsttafel*, meaning 'rice table'. The different textures, colours, flavours and levels of spiciness were the most exotic and awesome thing I had ever tasted. In later years, I was introduced to salt-preserved herring that I'd knock back in the morning to cure my hangover. So, yes, I guess you could say that pickled and fermented foods are very much a part of the kind of food I grew up eating, and essentially became a core part of any meal for me.

Fast-forward to 2008, when I moved to London, then travelled to Singapore, Mexico, Malaysia, Japan, Vietnam, the US, Australia and South Africa, ate at a ton of amazing restaurants and market stalls. Having been introduced to such mind-blowing and diverse food cultures, I felt inspired to understand my own journey and to give my take on the food I loved from my childhood.

People tend to be intimidated by pickling and fermenting. They think there are lots of rules and percentages that you need to know about. Trust me, you don't. You also don't need to spend hours hunting out impossible-to-find specialist equipment because you'll probably have pretty much everything you need somewhere in your kitchen cupboard.

The majority of the recipes in this book are refrigerator pickles. These are made by soaking (mostly) raw, fresh ingredients in a vinegar-based brine with sugar and salt, and often flavoured with spices or herbs. Now for the science bit: the salt pulls out the moisture, meaning that bacteria stands no chance of developing, and the vinegar helps to preserve the natural crunch of your fruit and vegetables by stopping bacteria growing through its acidity. Because the pickles aren't cooked or fermented, it's a super-quick method for making crunchy delights such as Pickled Nashi Pear (see page 31), Rosemary Pickled Plums (see page 36), Thai Shallots (see page 19) and Szechuan Pickled Watermelon (see page 23). There are also recipes for properly fermented vegetables with salt-based brines, and a few different kimchis.

The awesome thing about pickling is how humble ingredients (vinegar, salt or sugar, and fresh produce) transform into something extraordinary. You simply combine the ingredients, and then wait – either a couple of hours or a few months – for the magic to happen. The results will amaze you and your taste buds.

A little pickle can easily brighten up a meal with its crunchy texture and zingy freshness. Add chopped Thai Shallots (see page 19) to a curry, some F.A.T Sesame Kimchi (see page 73) to a grilled cheese sandwich (see page 121), your own homemade sriracha sauce (see page 86) to a burger, or serve your friends an assorted plate of pickles alongside cured meats and cheese (see page 20). Before you know it you'll be going by the name of 'Pickle Queen' (or King, obvs), as you'll want to pickle everything in sight – trust me.

On becoming #foodserious

I spent four years as a creative director at a London boutique advertising agency, Protein, where I worked with some amazing clients. One career highlight was working at an event alongside Dante Gonzales, a chef from the States known for throwing these amazing music and food parties in his loft in Brooklyn. He whipped up his infamous fried chicken for the masses while I manned the salad station. That was my first day at the agency, so it was a pretty weird but good first day. Following that, my job allowed me to travel to places like Miami, New York, LA and Boston, to work and film with incredibly creative and inspiring teams and, more importantly, to eat out in all these insane cities, which ultimately pushed me towards my new career.

During my time in 'ad land', I'd always toyed around with the idea of doing something in food. I started a pop-up called F.A.T, named after me, Freddie, and my friends Alice Waese, an artist and designer, and Terence Teh, a journalist – both are now based in New York. The three of us loved food. We nerded out together over Anthony Bourdain books and TV shows. Though, if you dared call us foodies we'd give you a death stare, as of course we weren't.

(I guess we totally were.) We started off hosting dinners in the gallery at Protein, which later turned into pop-ups, street parties and a handful of catering events. Most of the time, we didn't know what the hell we were doing. None of us had worked in the restaurant industry before and all of a sudden, we were in a room of 100 people trying to order ten different things from a menu that we'd literally just come up with, and had never even cooked before. We were massively winging it. But I think it was that feeling of stepping into the unknown, with really good friends, doing something different, something we believed in, that made it real. And it's the buzz I got out of it – serving people new food and unfamiliar flavours, creating a vibe that felt exciting and new – that ultimately made me want to pursue a career in food.

I eventually left my job at Protein to make the move into the great big world of food. I started out running a three-month pop-up lunch counter inside a coffee shop, which also functioned as a barbershop – you know, one of those cool, quirky, multifunctional places. I thought it would be incredibly hard to start something from scratch. I'd left the daily grind of sitting behind my laptop for ten hours and instead found myself running around the entire city to butchers, bakeries, markets; writing menus; and cooking every day from early in the morning to late at night. I didn't know anyone in the industry or how to source good fruit and veg suppliers, and so placed very small orders at independent producers who didn't do delivery. The first day, my friend James Lowe came over – he's now owner, head chef (and my boss) at Lyle's, a Michelin-starred restaurant in London. He hooked me up with Justin Gellatly, who created London's St John Bakery and the restaurant's infamous sourdough bread and doughnuts (and now runs the amazing Bread Ahead Bakery in London) and he brought me weekly batches of homemade ketchup. I was just about to serve my first customer when he pulled me aside to tell me I really needed to wear an apron if I wanted to be taken seriously by anyone that worked in food. My first thought was that I'd look like I was trying to be someone I wasn't if I did, so I ignored James's advice. I rocked up in fun outfits every day that week until all of a sudden food bloggers and a couple of chefs were dropping in. That's when I put on an apron and shit got real. I became #foodserious.

A little later, my friends opened their first restaurant, Rita's, and they asked if I could be their pickles and kimchi supplier. Then another friend, Lillie O'Brien of the beautiful London Borough of Jam, asked if I wanted to sell some of my pickles and condiments in her shop, which finally happened once I'd figured out how to bottle and label everything properly. I wanted my food to taste good but also look good. I guess that's the marketing and advertising background in me.

Fast-forward a couple of years and I'm now running a stall at the weekend, serving grilled cheese sandwiches with homemade pickles at the fantastic Druid Street Market in South London. As my day job, I do restaurant marketing and PR. I never, ever would have imagined I'd write a book, but I guess it's here now, and I don't think it can get more serious than this.

Some pretty cool facts

1 The word pickle comes from the Dutch word *pekel*, which means brine.

2 Although pickling and fermenting is super cool right now, both are actually an ancient process that started for many reasons: to preserve food (before refrigeration), to produce alcohol, or simply to add flavour. Mostly it came out of the necessity to have seasonal produce available all year long.

3 When fermenting food, you are transforming microorganisms like bacteria and yeast, as well as the enzymes they produce. Fermented food is mad healthy and really good for your gut. Basically, eating kimchi and sauerkraut makes you an all-round good person.

4 By contrast, eating pickles that are preserved in vinegar-brine with sugar (and salt and spices) is, admittedly, not the healthiest thing in the world. However, if you make the pickles yourself, you are in control of the amount of sugar. This way at least you know what you're eating, which isn't always the case with the store-bought stuff.

5 We eat fermented foods all the time: sourdough bread, olives, yoghurt, cheese, wine, beer, vinegar ... the list goes on.

6 If you really want to get down with the fermentation kids, read Sandor Katz's *The Art of Fermentation* – he's the ultimate fermenting king.

Pickling vs Fermenting

What's the difference between pickling and fermenting? Not all pickles are fermented and not all fermented foods are pickled.

In short, pickling is the process of preserving a food in an acidic medium, usually vinegar (which in itself is a product of fermentation). That's it. With pickling, raw or lightly cooked ingredients are often immersed in hot brine, which has the effect of diminishing the nutrients. This means that unlike fermented foods, pickles don't actually give you that probiotic health boost.

Fermenting, on the other hand, actually creates nutrients, including good bacteria that are super-good for you. With some salt, filtered water and sometimes a starter, you can convert sugar into acids. This can only happen in an oxygen-starved space, which is why people use special fermenting crocks, where the food is pressed down as much as possible, to eliminate or minimise the amount of air bubbles. During fermentation the food will create its own acidic liquid. This liquid is called lactic acid and the process that produces it is called 'lacto-fermentation'. This process first kills off harmful bacteria, after which it begins to convert lactose and other sugars in the food into lactic acid, which preserves the food safely, and also gives it that nice zingy flavour. Think kimchi, sauerkraut, and yoghurt – probiotic foods that are not exposed to heat and create their own acidic liquid, and are really good for your gut.

Fermentation halts (or slows down) the growth of microorganisms, after which it encourages the growth of bacteria, mould and yeasts. Basically, a fermented food is 'alive' as the culture continues to develop over time. Keep this in mind when storing your kimchi and sauerkraut; their flavour profiles will transform the longer you leave them and it's up to you to decide how you like them – so keep tasting and testing them until you're happy with both the taste and texture.

Tips for awesome results

Fresh Produce
Buy the nicest, freshest, most seasonal produce you can. If a cucumber looks soft and limp, it's not all of a sudden going to taste fresh and delicious and be crunchy as hell when you pickle it. If you choose seasonal ingredients they will be at their best. All you need to do is treat them well by preserving them properly, and I guarantee that your pickles will taste great.

Garlic
Don't freak out if the garlic in your brine turns bright blue. It might look like some sort of scary chemical reaction, but it just means that the garlic is old. It won't harm the pickle.

Salt
Salt draws out water from the vegetable or fruit you're using, which then creates an environment where bad bacteria die, and good bacteria can grow. It's important to use good salt, such as kosher, sea or pickling salt, rather than normal table salt. This contains caking agents like iodine, which can cloud the brines and inhibit beneficial bacteria during fermentation.

Spices
Avoid buying ready-made pickling bags. It is better to experiment and add your own spices. If you're worried about the spices floating around in the brine, and having to pick them out one by one before serving, put the spices in a small muslin (cheesecloth) bag and tie it with butcher's string.

Sugar
Sugar acts as both a preserver and a flavour enhancer. With pickles, it also helps to balance out the acidity from the vinegar. Normal, granulated (raw) sugar is absolutely fine – you can use caster (superfine) sugar as well (it dissolves quicker) but by all means, regular white sugar that you'll find in any kitchen in a sugar bowl is sufficient.

Vinegar
Don't use cheap vinegar. You will taste it. I use apple cider vinegar, red wine vinegar, white wine vinegar and my personal favourite, rice wine vinegar. Rice wine vinegar has a lower acetic acid content, which means ingredients will take longer to pickle in it, leading to a less harsh and, well, less vinegary taste. The type of vinegar you use for preserving will vary your end result in terms of colour and taste.

You can of course make your own vinegars, but if you are new to pickling it is probably easier to buy them. If you want try something different, you can make flavoured vinegar by infusing it with things like shiso, liquorice or elderflower (see page 55). It's totally fine to reuse a vinegar-brine once or twice. Make sure it has the right flavour profile that you're after though. If you want to reuse a vinegar-brine, simply strain it, reheat it, taste for sweetness, saltiness and spices and pour it over your pickles.

A few things about equipment (and how little you really need)

For measuring
My one piece of advice regarding equipment is: get yourself a good set of measuring tools, teaspoons, tablespoons, etc., and stick to them.

For pickling
You don't need anything fancy, just a good heavy-based pan, ideally non-reactive or stainless steel, for heating up vinegars. You'll also need glass jars with tight-fitting vinegar-proof lids (such as Mason jars) and food-grade plastic jars for storing pickles and condiments.

For fermenting
If you're just starting out with fermentations, you can make do with whatever you have at home. Just follow these tips:

* Have a look at the 'makes' amount at the start of the recipe and have the right-sized jar or container ready. It's best to be on the big side of big not the small side of big so that the fermentation can do its thing. It's going to fizz and bubble so it needs space to 'burp'.
* It's a good idea to place the jar or container on a plate during fermentation in case any liquid bubbles over. This is important when making very active things like sauerkraut and hot sauces (such as sriracha and kimchi hot sauce) that can both fizz and burp quite a bit!
* Avoid using metal jars, bowls or containers. Use vessels made from non-reactive materials such as ceramics and food-grade plastic containers.
* Always make sure you cover the ingredients fully in the brine. The best way to do this is to press down on it completely, releasing all the bubbles from the liquid, then put a clean plate on top followed by something heavy to keep it submerged in the liquid. I've found a zip-lock bag filled with water works pretty well as a weight.

If you really want to get serious about fermenting, invest in a ceramic sauerkraut crock. They have fitted lids with weights and also airlocks, which is pretty snazzy and efficient.

Sterilising, potting and storage
When preserving, always use a sterilised jar. You don't want anything getting contaminated. If you're making a refrigerator pickle, which won't keep longer than a few days, simply washing your jar in very hot, soapy water will do the trick. If you're looking to store the preserve for a couple of weeks or longer, there are two options. You can wash the jars, including their lids, in hot water and soap and then place them in a preheated oven for about 10 minutes, until the jars and lids are completely dry. Or you can dump the jars and lids in your dishwasher on the hottest setting.

Make sure when potting that the ingredients are at the same temperature as the jar, otherwise you'll risk spoilage. For example, add hot liquids to hot jars, and add room temperature liquids to, yes, room temperature jars. Simple. Never fill to the top, always leave a bit of space for it to breathe. Once you've added your ingredients, close the jar or container straight away, leave to cool to room temperature and then refrigerate.

PICKLES

I remember the first time I pickled something – it was baby cucumbers and they tasted rank. It makes me laugh now because pickling cucumbers is so easy.

When it comes to pickles, you don't need to be a superstar chef. There's really not much effort when it comes to pickling – there's much more effort happening inside the jar. And I honestly believe that if you have a few jars of homemade pickles in your fridge, you're always prepared for an impromptu dinner party, or even a casual weeknight meal – the addition of these big flavours can uplift any simple meal or snack.

Cucumber pickles are really easy to make and go with pretty much everything. Once you've tried them, you'll want to make sure you always have a jar of these guys in the fridge, trust me. I eat them straight from the jar, work them into a potato salad or salsa verde and, of course, they're ace with a grilled cheese sandwich. You can also cut them into chips (I like crinkle cut), and they're wicked in a burger.

Cucumber Dill Pickles

750 g (1 lb 10 oz) pickling
* cucumbers, rinsed and*
* quartered*
1 bunch of dill
1–2 garlic cloves, peeled
* and thinly sliced*
pared zest of ½ lemon
250 ml (8½ fl oz) rice wine
* vinegar*
250 ml (8½ fl oz) white wine
* vinegar*
100 g (3½ oz/½ cup)
* granulated (raw) sugar*
2 tablespoons sea salt
1 tablespoon yellow
* mustard seeds*
1 tablespoon black
* peppercorns*
¼ cinnamon stick
pinch of chilli flakes

Makes 1 × 1 litre (34 fl oz) jar

1 Put your quartered cucumbers and the dill into a large, clean jar or plastic container.
2 Drop in the sliced garlic and lemon zest.
3 In a large saucepan, combine the remaining ingredients, plus 250 ml (8½ fl oz) of water, and simmer over a medium to high heat. Make sure to stir it constantly for about 10 minutes, until your sugar is fully dissolved.
4 Turn off the heat and allow the pickling liquid to cool for around 5 minutes.
5 Pour the warm liquid over your cucumbers, making sure they're fully submerged. If need be, you can use a plate to weigh the cucumbers down as you fill the jar. Put the lid on the jar or container and refrigerate. The pickles will be tasty in 1–2 days, but they will be awesome in a week's time. You can keep them, chilled, for up to 3 weeks, but after this time they will lose some of their crunch.

These make such an awesome snack with an ice-cold beer, or serve them as part of a Thai curry. If you wanna go all out and kill it on the bar snacks front, roast up some peanuts or pork scratchings with a bit of fish sauce, salt, pepper, sugar and kaffir lime powder.
Serve with these babies, and you're #WINNING.

Thai Shallots

200 g (7 oz) shallots
   (around 8–10), unpeeled
250 ml (8½ fl oz) rice wine
   vinegar
220 g (8 oz/1 cup) granulated
   (raw) sugar
1 tablespoon sea salt
5 fresh kaffir lime leaves
½ lemongrass stalk

Makes 1 × 500 ml (17 fl oz) jar

1 Place the unpeeled shallots in a large bowl and cover with boiling water. Leave to sit for 1 minute. Drain and allow to cool.
2 When the shallots are cool enough to handle, peel them and set aside.
3 Bring the vinegar, sugar and salt to the boil in a pan and whisk over medium heat, until the sugar has dissolved.
4 Add the peeled shallots to the pan along with the kaffir lime leaves and lemongrass, bring it back up to the boil, and simmer over medium to low heat for 5 minutes.
5 Use a slotted spoon to remove the shallots, lemongrass and lime leaves and place in a clean jar.
6 Bring the vinegar-brine back up to the boil, and cook over medium heat for another 5 minutes.
7 Carefully pour the hot pickling brine over the shallots. Put the lid on and allow to cool, then refrigerate. The pickles will be ready in 2 days and will keep for up to 1 month in the fridge.

I absolutely love the salty sea flavour of samphire – steamed, with butter and served with fish – yum. It's only in season for a short amount of time so, I figured, why not pickle it and make it last a little longer? Because of its very salty nature, you don't use any salt in the making of the brine. Serve it with fish, a lobster roll, or as part of a charcuterie board.

Pickled Samphire

250 g (9 oz) samphire
250 ml (8½ fl oz) rice wine
   vinegar
250 ml (8½ fl oz) cider
   vinegar
50 g (2 oz/¼ cup) granulated
   (raw) sugar
2 bay leaves
1 teaspoon mustard seeds
½ teaspoon coriander seeds
½ teaspoon black peppercorns

Makes 1 × 500 ml (17 fl oz) jar

1 Bring a pan of water to the boil and add the samphire. Blanch for 10 seconds, then plunge in ice-cold water, and drain.

2 Next, put the remaining ingredients in a medium-sized pan. Set over medium heat and stir until the sugar has dissolved. Take off the heat and allow to cool completely.

3 Put the samphire in a clean jar and pour in the cooled vinegar-brine, making sure all the samphire is submerged. Put the lid on and refrigerate. The pickles will be ready in 2 days and will keep for up to 2 weeks in the fridge.

Clockwise from the top:
Pickled Samphire (above),
Coffee Pickle Pour Over
Mushrooms (see page
25), Szechuan Pickled
Watermelon (see page 23)

A sweet and fragrant Southern pickle with an Asian twist. It works great with salty, meaty things like pork chops, bacon and charcuterie. Or do like Chloe from Fatties Bakery in London – she eats them straight out of the jar in front of the TV after a long day of making those yummy salted caramels I'm addicted to.

Szechuan Pickled Watermelon

½ watermelon
250 ml (8½ fl oz) rice wine
   vinegar
220 g (8 oz/1 cup) granulated
   (raw) sugar
1 tablespoon sea salt
2 star anise
1 thumb-sized piece
   fresh ginger, peeled
1 tablespoon Szechuan
   peppercorns
1 cinnamon stick

Makes 1 × 500 ml (17 fl oz) jar

1 First, prepare the watermelon by cutting it into quarters. Using a sharp knife, remove the tough green peel. Cut the rind into 2 cm (1 in) wedges, then slice the wedges into small bite-sized squares. Reserve the watermelon flesh for a salad, drink or just a snack.
2 In a large pan, combine 125 ml (4 fl oz) of water with the rest of the ingredients. Place over a medium to high heat and warm through. Do not allow it to boil.
3 Add the watermelon rind to the pan, boil for 1 minute, then simmer for another 5 minutes.
4 Take off the heat and transfer the watermelon to a clean jar or plastic container. Put the lid on, leave to cool and then refrigerate. Once the pickles have cooled down they're ready to eat. Store in your fridge for up to 1 week.

These are delicious and earthy, sweet, umami-rich mushrooms. I made these with my friend James 'Beans' Low, who is a coffee genius. As the head barista at Lyle's, he's managed to take restaurant coffee in the UK to the next level with a specialty coffee service, sourcing hard-to-find, interesting coffee from companies such as Koppi, Belleville and JB Kaffee. Serve these pickles as part of a charcuterie plate, slice them up and add to a pizza or sandwich, or fry them in a bit of olive oil and eat with scrambled eggs.

Coffee Pickle Pour Over Mushrooms

100 g (3½ oz/1 cup) dried
*   shiitake mushrooms*
125 ml (4 fl oz) white wine
*   vinegar*
1½ tablespoons granulated
*   (raw) sugar*
1 tablespoon freshly ground
*   coffee beans*

Makes 1 × 300 ml (10 fl oz) jar

1 Place the dried mushrooms in a bowl and cover with 500 ml (17 fl oz) of boiling water. Put a plate on top of the mushrooms to push them down into the water, making sure they are submerged. Soak for 15 minutes.
2 Strain the mushrooms through a fine mesh colander, reserving 125 ml (4 fl oz) of the soaking liquid.
3 In a pan, combine the mushroom liquid with the vinegar and sugar and bring to 92°C (197.5°F), not boiling, stirring, until the sugar is completely dissolved and the temperature reads 90°C (194°F). You don't want the mixture to get any hotter, otherwise you will burn the coffee.
4 Put the mushrooms into a clean jar or plastic container.
5 Add the ground coffee beans to a lined filter (I use a ceramic V60 coffee dripper) and place it over the jar or container with the mushrooms.
6 Slowly pour a small amount (around 50 ml/2 fl oz) of the pickling liquid over the coffee grounds and leave for 30 seconds.
7 Now add the remaining liquid to the filter until it fills the jar or container.
8 Let it come to room temperature before putting on the lid and refrigerating. The pickles will be ready to eat in 1 day and keep for up to 2 weeks when refrigerated.

For this recipe, use a V60 coffee dripper or similar ceramic coffee filter to pour the pickling liquid into the coffee grounds.

This is the sweet, crunchy daikon and carrot pickle that's traditionally served with banh mi. They add an awesome crunch to the Vietnamese sandwich, and to me are just as important as all the other ingredients on there. You can also serve the pickle alongside steamed rice, with grilled meat, or in a salad.

Banh Mi Pickles

250 g (9 oz) carrots, peeled and cut into fine matchsticks
250 g (9 oz) daikon (mooli) radish, peeled and cut into fine matchsticks
3 teaspoons sea salt
125 ml (4 fl oz) rice wine vinegar
55 g (2 oz/¼ cup) granulated (raw) sugar

Makes 1 × 300 ml (10 fl oz) jar

1 Combine the carrots, daikon radish and 1 teaspoon of sea salt in a colander, scrunch it into the vegetables and let it sit for 30 minutes.
2 Rinse the vegetables, then pat dry with a kitchen towel.
3 Place the vegetables in a clean jar or plastic container.
4 In large bowl, combine 125 ml (4 fl oz) of warm water with the vinegar, sugar and the remaining salt until they have completely dissolved.
5 Pour the pickling liquid over the vegetables in the jar or container. Put the lid on and refrigerate. Your pickles will be ready to eat in 1 hour and will keep for up to 2 weeks in the fridge.

Beetroot and horseradish – it's a classic combo and works amazingly well served with smoked fish and cured meat. I like to slice the beetroot into chips so you can add them to a sandwich; it's banging on rye bread with smoked mackerel, or in a salt beef bagel. There's definitely a kick to these pickles, so don't forget when grating the horseradish to make sure you're in a well-ventilated area, otherwise you'll end up crying from its pungent scent.

Wasabi Beets

250 g (9 oz) candy or regular
  beetroot (beets), peeled,
  rinsed and leaves removed
1 tablespoon sea salt
4 teaspoons granulated (raw)
  sugar
1 teaspoon chilli flakes
2 teaspoons freshly
  grated ginger

for the prepared horseradish:
100 g (3½ oz) horseradish,
  coarsely grated
150 ml (5 fl oz) white wine
  vinegar
½ teaspoon sea salt

Makes 1 × 300 ml (10 fl oz) jar

1 Make the prepared horseradish by putting the horseradish, half of the vinegar and salt in a food processor. Blitz until the horseradish breaks down.
2 Add the remaining vinegar and 3 tablespoons of water, a spoon at a time, until you have a paste. If it's too watery, strain out some of the liquid.
3 Set aside 2 tablespoons of the prepared horseradish for the beetroot. Transfer the rest to a clean jar, put the lid on and store in the fridge, where it will keep for 3–4 weeks.
4 Slice the beetroot on a mandoline into evenly-sized discs and put in a bowl along with the reserved prepared horseradish, salt, sugar, chilli flakes and ginger.
5 Put on some disposable gloves, and use your hands to work the horseradish into the beetroot.
6 Transfer to a clean jar and place something heavy on top to squash the beetroot down. Leave to rest for 1 hour. Stir, and your wasabi beets are ready to eat.

Us Dutch people go loco for liquorice! It's one of my favourite flavours. Also, its aniseed taste really complements the earthiness and sweetness of the beets.

Liquorice Pickled Beetroot

500 g (1 lb 2 oz) beetroot,
  (beets) rinsed and leaves
  removed
300 ml (10 fl oz) white wine
  vinegar
3 liquorice roots, broken
  into pieces
1 shallot, thinly sliced
100 g (3½ oz/½ cup)
  granulated (raw) sugar
5 black peppercorns
1 teaspoons sea salt

Makes 1 × 500 ml (17 fl oz) jar

1 Fill a medium-sized pan with water and bring to the boil. Add the beetroot, reduce the heat, and simmer for about 1–2 hours, until tender.
2 Drain the beetroot and allow to cool completely.
3 Put the remaining ingredients in a separate pan with 100 ml (3½ fl oz) of water. Bring to the boil, then reduce to a low heat and cook for around 30 minutes.
4 Peel the skins off the cooled beetroot, chop into bite-sized chunks and place into a clean jar.
5 Bring the vinegar-brine liquid in the pan to a slight simmer, then pour into the jar, submerging the beetroot completely.
6 Allow to cool to room temperature, put the lid on the jar and refrigerate. Your pickles will be ready to eat in 2–3 days and will keep for up to 2 weeks.

I love pickled fennel: it's crunchy, sweet, aniseed-y, fresh. It's ace as part of a pickle plate, or – if cut very thinly – as a base for a salad, but I serve them in my Ultimate Meatball Sandwich (see page 97).

Sweet Fennel Pickles

2 fennel bulbs
125 ml (4 fl oz) rice wine
vinegar
125 ml (4 fl oz) white wine
vinegar
1 tablespoon sea salt
3 tablespoons granulated
(raw) sugar
1 teaspoon coriander seeds
1 teaspoon fennel seeds

Makes 2 × 300 ml (10 fl oz) jars

1 Rinse the fennel bulbs and remove the stalks. Cut the fennel into thin slivers and put them into a clean jar or plastic container.
2 Combine the vinegars, salt, sugar and 125 ml (4 fl oz) of water in a medium-sized pan and continue to simmer over a medium to high heat.
3 Add the coriander and fennel seeds and simmer over medium to high heat for 5 minutes.
4 Pour the hot pickling liquid over the fennel in the jar. Put the lid on, then cool and refrigerate. Your pickles will be ready to eat in 5 days and will keep for up to 2 weeks in the fridge.

These pickled nashi pears will blow your mind! Combined with the incredibly delicious Stilton Dip (see page 81), they are perfect as part of a pickle plate, in a salad or as a side with ribs or any barbecued meats.

Pickled Nashi Pear

2 Asian nashi pears
250 ml (8½ fl oz) rice wine
vinegar
220 g (8 oz/1 cup) granulated
(raw) sugar
1 teaspoon sea salt
1 garlic clove, peeled and
thinly sliced

Makes 2 × 300 ml (10 fl oz) jars

1 Rinse the pears, peel, quarter, remove the core and chop into wedges. Set aside.
2 Combine the vinegar, sugar and salt in a medium-sized pan over a medium to high heat. Stir until the sugar dissolves, add the pear and toss until coated.
3 Fill another medium-sized pan with water and simmer over a medium to high heat. Remove the pears from the vinegar-brine, place them in the water and cook for around 5 minutes – they should still be crunchy.
4 Remove the pears from the water and put them in a clean jar. Add the garlic.
5 Reduce the vinegar-brine to a syrup by cooking it for 5 minutes over medium to high heat.
6 Pour the syrup over the pears, put on the lid, let them cool to room temperature and refrigerate. They will be ready to eat in 3 days and will keep for up to 2 weeks in the fridge.

ckwise from top left:
achi Butter (see page 82),
ton Dip (see page 81),
nge Blossom Carrots
e page 43), Bourbon
kled Okra (see page 32),
cumber Dill Pickles (see
e 17), Pickled Nashi Pear
e right), Sweet Fennel
kles (see above), Rose
dishes (see page 43)

Bourbon Pickled Okra

200 g (7 oz) okra
250 ml (8½ fl oz) rice wine
  vinegar
250 ml (8½ fl oz) cider vinegar
2 tablespoons granulated
  (raw) sugar
4 tablespoons sea salt
2 tablespoons yellow
  mustard seeds
1 teaspoon coriander seeds
½ teaspoon black
  peppercorns
125 ml (4 fl oz) bourbon
1 tablespoon chilli flakes
4 fresh dill sprigs
3 garlic cloves, peeled
  and thinly sliced
pared zest of ½ lemon

Makes 2 × 300 ml (10 fl oz) jars

1 Rinse the okra, trim and discard the stems.
2 Combine the vinegars, sugar, salt and 250 ml (8½ fl oz) of water in a medium-sized pan, whisking over a medium to high heat until the sugar and salt have completely dissolved.
3 Add the mustard and coriander seeds, peppercorns, bourbon and chilli, and simmer for 5 minutes.
4 Put the okra, dill, garlic and lemon zest in a clean jar or plastic container.
5 Pour the hot pickling brine over the okra. Put on the lid and let it cool completely, then refrigerate. The pickles will be ready to eat in 2 days and will keep for up to 2 weeks in the fridge.

If you don't like okra because of its sometimes 'slimy' texture, try pickling it! It's seriously amazing – it becomes super crunchy and yummy.

I think all of us go to a dirty kebab shop every now and then, right? At least I'd like to think so – it makes me feel less like a bad person. My guilty pleasure is a lamb durum, with extra pickled chillies – you just can't have a kebab, or a falafel, without those awesome Turkish chillies. This is my homemade version, which I add to my Sourdough Flatbread with Cumin Lamb & Kebab Chillies recipe (see page 105).

Kebab Chillies

300 g (10½ oz) long
  green chillies
1 garlic clove, peeled
1 thyme sprig
350 ml (12 fl oz) cider vinegar
2 tablespoons sea salt
150 g (5 oz/⅔ cup) granulated
  (raw) sugar
¼ teaspoon paprika
¼ teaspoon freshly ground
  black pepper

Makes 1 × 750 ml (25 fl oz) jar

1 Rinse the chillies and put them in a clean jar with the garlic and thyme.
2 Combine the vinegar, 350 ml (12 fl oz) of water, the salt, sugar, paprika and black pepper in a medium-sized pan, and stir until the salt and sugar have dissolved.
3 Take off the heat and immediately pour the hot vinegar-brine over the chillies. Put the lid on and allow to cool. Refrigerate for 2 weeks before using. These will keep for up to 3 months in the fridge.

My friend Magnus Reid, who runs London's C.R.E.A.M cafe (see page 113), has brought me some awesome finds after foraging trips and farm visits – mushrooms, horseradish leaves (which are great for keeping your pickles crunchy) and plums, LOTS of them. They were gorgeous, but right at the tail end of their life, perfect for pickling and preserving. So I figured, #WeCanPickleThat. You can add these pickles, sliced, to a nice hearty salad, they go incredibly well with a cheese plate or you can bring the entire jar with you to a barbecue party and everyone will love you.

Rosemary Pickled Plums

250 g (9 oz) red plums
½ cinnamon stick
2 rosemary sprigs
500 ml (17 fl oz) cider vinegar
220 g (8 oz/1 cup) granulated
(raw) sugar
½ tablespoon sea salt

Makes 1 × 750 ml (25 fl oz) jar

1 Rinse the plums carefully. Place them in a clean jar or plastic container.
2 Add the cinnamon and rosemary sprigs.
3 Bring the vinegar, sugar and salt to the boil in a medium-sized pan. Cook over medium to high heat, whisking until the sugar has dissolved.
4 Pour the hot pickling brine over the plums in the jar. Let it cool to room temperature, then put the lid on and refrigerate. The pickles will be ready to eat in 5 days and keep for up to 2 months in the fridge.

Cardamom Pickled Greengages

10 cardamom pods
250 g (9 oz) greengages
½ cinnamon stick
2 star anise
500 ml (17 fl oz) cider vinegar
220 g (8 oz/1 cup) granulated
(raw) sugar
½ tablespoon sea salt

Makes 1 × 750 ml (25 fl oz) jar

1 Gently bash the cardamom pods to reveal their seeds. Pick them out and discard the pods.
2 Rinse the greengages carefully. Place them in a clean jar or plastic container.
3 Add the reserved cardamom seeds, cinnamon and star anise to the jar.
4 Bring the vinegar, sugar and salt to the boil in a medium-sized pan. Cook over medium to high heat, whisking until the sugar has dissolved.
5 Pour the hot pickling brine over the greengages and spices in the jar. Let it cool to room temperature, then put the lid on and refrigerate. The pickles will be ready to eat in 5 days and keep for up to 2 months in the fridge.

You can find these pickles at pretty much every *taqueria* and taco stand in Yucatán, Mexico. They're super easy to make and are a great addition to tacos, sandwiches, burgers, hot dogs as well as fresh seafood. I like to serve them with my Chipotle Pork Tacos with Yucatán Pickles on page 110.

Yucatán Pickles

2 red onions, thinly sliced
2 teaspoons sea salt
375 ml (12½ fl oz) red wine
    vinegar
1 teaspoon black peppercorns
1 garlic clove, peeled
    and crushed
2 teaspoons dried oregano

Makes 2 × 300 ml (10 fl oz) jars

1 Toss the onions and salt together in a bowl. Allow to sit for about 30 minutes, stirring every now and then, until the onions have started to release some liquid and are beginning to look nice and pink.
2 Add the vinegar, peppercorns, garlic and oregano, and mix well.
3 Transfer to a clean jar, put the lid on and chill for 3 hours before using. The pickles will keep in the fridge for up to 1 week.

These are fun and really easy to make, quick to rustle up, and great for impressing your friends at an impromptu dinner party, as they're so pretty and tasty. Serve them by themselves, or with steak, salads and tacos.

Party Quickles

250 ml (8½ fl oz) rice wine vinegar
250 ml (8½ fl oz) cider vinegar
220 g (8 oz/1 cup) granulated (raw) sugar
1 teaspoon sea salt
1 teaspoon freshly ground black pepper
1 teaspoon yellow mustard seeds
2 bunches of radishes (approx. 20 radishes), washed
large handful of carrot (approx. 6 carrots), washed
large bunch of fresh coriander (cilantro), finely chopped
small handful of red chillies (approx. 5 chillies)

Makes 1 × 750 ml (25 fl oz) jar

1 Combine the vinegars, sugar, salt and 250 ml (8½ fl oz) of water in a large pan and bring to the boil. Whisk over medium to high heat, until all the sugar has dissolved. Add the black pepper and mustard seeds. Take off the heat and allow to cool to room temperature.
2 Slice the radishes and carrots into very thin round discs on a mandoline (you could do this with a sharp knife, trying to get the slices as thin as you can).
3 Toss the radishes and carrots in a bowl with the coriander. Place into a clean jar.
4 Slice the chillies into small round discs, about the same thickness as the radish and carrot and add them to the jar.
5 Pour the cooled pickling brine over the sliced vegetables and herbs. Put the lid on and refrigerate. The pickles will be ready to eat in a few hours, and keep for up to 1 week in the fridge.

Rose water and orange blossom water are awesome and can bring a huge amount of beautiful flavour to very simple things. Just remember to add tiny amounts as too much can easily leave a soapy taste.

Orange Blossom Carrots

120 ml (4 fl oz) rice wine
  vinegar
120 ml (4 fl oz) cider vinegar
100 g (3½ oz/½ cup)
  granulated (raw) sugar
1 teaspoon sea salt
few drops of orange
  blossom water
large handful of carrots
  (approx. 6 carrots), rinsed
  peeled and halved
  lengthways

Makes 1 × 500 ml (17 fl oz) jar

1 Combine the vinegars, sugar, salt and 120 ml (4 fl oz) of water in a large pan and bring to the boil. Whisk over a medium to high heat until all the sugar has dissolved. Add the orange blossom water.
2 Put the carrots into a clean jar and cover with the hot vinegar liquid.
3 Put the lid on, let cool to room temperature and refrigerate. The pickles will be ready to eat in 3 days and keep for up to 1 week.

To make Rose Radishes, follow the exact quantities and method as the recipe above but replace the carrots with 1 bunch of radishes (approx. 20 radishes) and the orange blossom water with a few drops of rose water.

When I moved to London eight years ago I spent many Sunday afternoons (ok, and Friday and Saturday nights) at pubs in east London, drinking pints, eating scampi fries, pork scratchings and salt and vinegar crisps (potato chips). A friend then opened me up to the world of pickled eggs. According to him, the only way to eat them is to drop the egg into a bag of crisps, shake it around, and consume with your beer. This is a jazzed up version of that, with chipotles added to the regular vinegar-brine, and tortilla chips instead of normal ones, because that makes the most sense if you're going for a Mexican-British hybrid snack. Serve to friends with ice-cold beers or Missy Flynn's Tepache (page 134).

Chipotle Pickled Eggs

10 medium eggs
500 ml (17 fl oz) cider vinegar
2 garlic cloves, peeled
1 white onion, quartered
1 tablespoon sea salt
2 tablespoons granulated
  (raw) sugar
5 tinned chipotle chillies
  in adobo sauce
2 dried chipotles, ground

Makes 10 eggs

1 Place the eggs in a medium-sized pan of water and bring to the boil. Cook over a medium to low heat for 7 minutes, then drain. Transfer to a bowl filled with ice-cold water to cool down.

2 Peel the eggs in the water (this will help to keep the egg whites perfectly smooth) and transfer to a clean jar.

3 Combine the vinegar, garlic, onion, salt, sugar, chillies in adobo sauce, ground dried chipotles and 500 ml (17 fl oz) of water in a pan and bring to the boil. Cook and simmer for about 30 minutes, over medium to high heat, until the onion is translucent.

4 Remove the vinegar-brine from the heat and immediately pour over the eggs in the jar to cover well. Put on the lid and let cool to room temperature, then refrigerate for 3 days before eating. The pickled eggs will keep for up to 1 week. Serve with a packet of your favourite crisps!

Varieties of this sweet-and-sour pickle appear in many guises across Asia. It's called *achat* in Thai cuisine, *acar* in Malaysia and Indonesia, and we call it *atjar* in Holland. Indonesian food is a huge part of Dutch cuisine, since the Netherlands and Indonesia shared colonial links. There are Indonesian restaurants everywhere and the food was very much a part of my growing up. My first job in a restaurant was as a waitress in a small Indonesian place in Maastricht. The way of eating lots of small, colourful dishes – some spicy, some not – served with white rice, pickles and different *sambals* (chilli sauces) was something I loved, and felt really exciting and exotic.

Atjar

1 teaspoon coriander seeds, toasted and ground
2 tablespoons sesame oil
3 garlic cloves, peeled and very finely chopped
1 thumb-sized piece of fresh ginger, grated
2 teaspoons turmeric
1 tablespoon sambal oelek (available in Asian food stores)
50 g (2 oz) granulated (raw) sugar
1½ tablespoons sea salt
375 ml (12½ fl oz) cider vinegar
1 medium-sized white cabbage, washed
1 medium-sized carrot, washed and peeled
½ head of medium sized cauliflower, washed
4 fresh red chillies, deseeded and finely chopped

Makes 1 × 1 litre (34 fl oz) jar

1 Heat the oil in a small pan and add the ground coriander seeds, garlic and ginger. Cook over a medium to high heat for 5 minutes, until aromatic and starting to turn golden.
2 Add the turmeric and *sambal oelek* to the pan and stir-fry for 3 minutes, until aromatic. Now add the sugar, salt, 375 ml (12½ fl oz) of water and the vinegar, and stir over a medium to high heat until all the sugar and salt have dissolved. Simmer for the next 5–10 minutes while you're prepping your veggies.
3 Cut the cabbage and carrot into very thin slices (use a mandoline if you have one). Cut the cauliflower into small florets.
4 Add all the vegetables to the pan with the chillies and cook for 5 minutes.
5 Drain the vegetable into a fine mesh sieve and discard the spices but reserve the pickling liquid. Put the pickles in a clean jar and top with the reserved liquid. Put the lid on and allow to cool to room temperature. Once cool, the pickles are ready to eat, but they will improve with age. If refrigerated, they will last for up to 1 month.

I remember having an amazing solo lunch at New York's Parm restaurant about five years ago where I ate these Italian pickles for the first time. Parm is an Italian-American diner set up by the same people behind the slightly more swanky Carbone, also in New York. When Parm opened, everyone went nuts for their meatball sub and turkey sandwich. Personally, I died when trying their *giardiniera* pickles. Pronounced 'jar-deen-yair-ah', the name means 'from the garden'. I love having them straight up as antipasti with cheese, cured meats and a good bottle of wine. But you can blitz them up into a salsa, or pile them on to sandwiches, hot dogs or, heck, why not a pizza?

Giardiniera Pickles

200 g (7 oz/¾ cup) sea salt
1 red (bell) pepper
1 yellow (bell) pepper
1 courgette (zucchini)
½ aubergine (eggplant)
100 g (3½ oz) button
  mushrooms
1 red onion
4 garlic cloves, peeled and
  thinly sliced
60 ml (2 fl oz) olive oil
2 rosemary sprigs
2 bay leaves
2 juniper berries
4 cloves
1 teaspoon black peppercorns
1 tablespoon granulated
  (raw) sugar
750 ml (25 fl oz) white wine
  vinegar

Makes 1 × 2 litre (3½ pint) jar

1 In a large tub or bowl, combine 2 litres (3½ pints) of water and the salt in a big tub and stir until dissolved.
2 Rinse and cut the peppers, courgette, aubergine, mushrooms and onion into your preferred shapes. I like adding a crinkle cut into the mix. Add them to the salt water.
3 Cover with a clean plate or something heavy to ensure everything is under water, and leave to sit overnight at room temperature.
4 The next day, drain the vegetables and rinse under cold water. Put on a tea towel to let them dry for 1–2 hours.
5 Add the drained and dried vegetables to a clean jar, along with the garlic, olive oil, rosemary, bay leaves, juniper berries, cloves, peppercorns, and sugar.
6 Top with the vinegar, press the vegetables down well, seal and store somewhere dark and cool. They will be ready in 1–2 weeks and keep, refrigerated after opening, for 1 month.

Japanese pickles, also called *tsukemono*, are served with pretty much every meal in Japan, and so are a massive part of the diet. Japanese pickling methods range from lightly salted cucumbers to heavily salted plums (*umeboshi*) to using mirin, sake, miso or soy as a pickling agent. This recipe is inspired by *shibazuke*, a pickle commonly served in Kyoto and made of aubergine, cucumber, purple shiso leaves, plum vinegar and *myoga* (shoots of ginger). My recipe is a casual, easy version. Serve with white rice or as a snack with an ice-cold beer.

Kyoto Pickles

3 Chinese (long) aubergines (eggplant)
1 pickling cucumber
good handful of purple shiso leaves (around 40)
2½ tablespoons sea salt
1 thumb-sized piece fresh ginger, cut into very thin matchsticks

Makes 1 × 500 ml (17 fl oz) jar

1 Rinse all your veg and the shiso leaves.
2 Put the shiso in a colander set inside a bowl and add ½ tablespoon salt. Use your hands to scrunch the salt into the shiso. Let it sit for 30 minutes, then squeeze the excess liquid from the shiso into the bowl.
3 Cut the aubergines and cucumber into long strips, about 5 mm (¼ in) thick. Soak the aubergine strips in a bowl of cold water to stop them from going brown.
4 Put the aubergines, cucumber and ginger in a bowl, sprinkle with the remaining salt, and let them sit for 30 minutes.
5 Now add the shiso leaves, along with the reserved liquid, and put everything into a clean jar. Add a weight on top and make sure it's tightly covered. If your vegetables aren't fully immersed in the liquid, add some water.
6 Refrigerate for about 1 week. Check every now and then – the vegetables will absorb some of the liquid, so give them a stir and add water if needed. Once ready, the pickles will keep in the fridge for 2 weeks.

These savoury, umami-packed pickles are made by covering vegetables in miso. You can use white miso for a slightly milder flavour. Miso is also a great way to preserve or marinate meat and fish.

Red Miso Aubergine Pickles

1 tablespoon sesame seeds
250 ml (8½ fl oz) red miso
60 ml (2 fl oz) mirin
1 tablespoon granulated (raw) sugar
1 tablespoon light soy sauce
10 baby aubergines (eggplant), cut into 5 cm (2 in) thick discs or cubes

Makes 1 × 500 ml (17 fl oz) jar

1 Combine the sesame seeds, miso, mirin, sugar and soy sauce in a large bowl.
2 Add the aubergines to the miso-mirin sauce and mix well to ensure all of the pieces are covered.
3 Transfer to a clean jar or plastic container, put on the lid and store in the fridge for 1 week, stirring every now and then.
4 When you're ready to dig in, remove the pickles from the jar, rinse them in cold water and serve. These will keep for up to 1 month.

Clockwise from top left: Pickled Mustard Greens (see page 53), Red Miso Aubergine (left), Shiso Quickles (see page 52), Daikon Kimchi (see page 66), F.A.T Kimchi Hot Sa (see page 74), Kyoto Pickles (above)

Quick pickles, or quickles, as the name suggests, only take a very short time to make. So for those that are worried about planning their dinners and accompanying pickles days or weeks in advance, don't you worry, you can make these in under an hour. This method works well with vegetables that have a high water content, such as cucumber, radish and onion. Just remember, the thinner you slice your vegetable, the quicker it will pickle!

Shiso Quickles

1 cucumber
1 tablespoon sea salt
125 ml (4 fl oz) Purple Shiso
  Vinegar (see page 55)
50 g (2 oz/¼ cup) granulated
  (raw) sugar

Makes 2 × 300 ml (10 fl oz) jars

1 Slice the cucumber into super-thin discs, using a mandoline. You want to be able to see through each slice. Alternatively, use a knife or use a vegetable peeler.
2 Place the cucumber slices in a bowl, add the salt and scrunch it in with your hands. Leave to sit for 10 minutes.
3 In a pan, mix 125 ml (4 fl oz) of water with the shiso vinegar and sugar and stir over a medium to high heat until the sugar has dissolved.
4 Pour the pickling brine over the cucumber and refrigerate for 10 minutes before eating. These will last for up to 1 week in the fridge.

When I lived in Chinatown for two years I spent a lot of time wandering around the Asian shops, and I became obsessed with their huge selections of vacuum-packed pickles. I'd always buy a couple of packs of different ones to try out. They're really cheap so it's worth giving them a go. My favourite one by far is Pickled Mustard Greens. They're salty, sour, sweet, crunchy – this is my homemade version. I make sure to always have some in the fridge as they're a key ingredient for making Dan Dan Noodles (recipe on page 100).

Pickled Mustard Greens

400 g (14 oz) mustard greens, ends trimmed and leaves rinsed
2 tablespoons sea salt
55 g (2 oz/¼ cup) granulated (raw) sugar
125 ml (4 fl oz) white wine vinegar
1 tablespoon Szechuan peppercorns
1 red chilli

Makes 1 × 500 ml (17 fl oz) jar

1 Bring a large pan of water to the boil over a high heat.
2 Add the greens to the boiling water – it will turn bright green. Blanch for 10 seconds, then drain and plunge into ice-cold water.
3 Gently squeeze the water out of the greens and set them aside in a bowl.
4 In a pan, whisk the salt, sugar and vinegar over a medium to high heat until the sugar has dissolved. Add the Szechuan peppercorns.
5 Put the greens and the chilli in a clean jar and pour over the vinegar-brine, making sure it is fully covered. Allow to cool completely, then refrigerate for 2 days before eating. These will last for up to 2 weeks in the fridge.

It's really easy to make your own herb-flavoured vinegars; these two are my favourite. You can use them for pickling veggies (see Shiso Quickles on page 52) or they make a nice and interesting change in a salad dressing too.

Elderflower Vinegar

15 elderflower heads
500 ml (17 fl oz) white wine
  vinegar

Makes 1 × 500 ml (17 fl oz)
  jar/bottle

1 If your elderflower heads are freshly picked, give them a good shake to discard any little bugs.
2 Pick the flowers from the stalks, pack them into a clean jar and cover them in the vinegar. Seal and refrigerate.
3 After 2 weeks, pour the vinegar through a fine mesh sieve or muslin into a sterilised jar or bottle and store in a dark, dry place. Discard the strained flowers. It will keep for up to 2 months.

Purple Shiso Vinegar

good handful of purple
  shiso leaves
500 ml (17 fl oz) rice wine
  vinegar

Makes 1 × 500 ml (17 fl oz)
  jar/bottle

1 Rinse the shiso leaves and chop them up roughly.
2 Place the leaves in a clean jar and add the rice wine vinegar. Seal and refrigerate.
3 After 3 days, pour the vinegar through a fine mesh sieve or muslin into a sterilised jar or bottle and store in a dark, dry place. Discard the strained leaves. It will keep for up to 2 months.

FERMENTATIONS

I used to be intimidated by fermenting. I thought it was a really technical process, and that I would need to buy lots of expensive equipment.

You don't.

Essentially, you put things in a jar, add some salt or water, push the air out and – ta-da! – you have made your own sauerkraut or kimchi. And it's super healthy for you, so eating these things make you a very good person!

Also called kosher dill pickles, these are made in the traditional manner of Jewish NYC pickle makers and are the ones you'll find in both classic and new-wave Jewish New York delis like Katz's, Mile End, and Russ & Daughters. Instead of being fermented in vinegar, the cucumbers are brined using a process of natural fermentation from salt brine, which makes them sour. There's your 'full-sour' pickles, which are fully fermented, and your 'half-sour', which are still crunchy, bright green and, as the name suggests, are half as sour. I prefer them half-sour, but all you need to do to make full-sours is leave them to ferment longer. The brine will get cloudier, and the colour will go a darker green.

NYC Deli Pickles

5 pickling cucumbers
3 tablespoons kosher salt or
   sea or sea salt
4–5 fresh dill sprigs
4 garlic cloves, peeled and
   smashed
1 tablespoon black
   peppercorns
1 tablespoon coriander seeds

Makes 1 × 1 litre (34 fl oz) jar

1 Rinse the cucumbers and soak them in ice-cold water for 1 hour.
2 Combine 1 litre (34 fl oz) of water with the salt, stirring until the salt has completely dissolved.
3 Pack as many of the cucumbers into a sterilised glass jar as you can. Top with the dill, garlic, peppercorns and coriander seeds.
4 Pour over the salt water, making sure the cucumbers are all fully submerged. Place a clean plate on top to weigh the cucumbers down if you need to. Put the lid on the jar and leave in a dark place for between 1–7 days to ferment.
5 Taste the brine each day to see when the pickles are to your taste. When they are how you like them, refrigerate them. The longer you leave the pickles to ferment, the more sour they'll taste. I'd say my preferred time is around 3 days. These will keep well, refrigerated, for 1 month.

Sauerkraut is a crunchy, sour and healthy condiment made entirely from cabbage and salt via the process of lactic acid fermentation and the aid of kindly bacteria. Not only are these bacteria good for your gut and immune system, sauerkraut is heaving with vitamins and minerals. You can buy special fermenting crocks for this process, but I find using what you have is normally fine, especially when you're just starting out and don't want to spend money unnecessarily. This kraut is the perfect garnish for a hot dog, topped with Umami Ketchup (see page 77) and Pickled Mustard Seeds (see page 85).

Proper Kraut

1 kg (2 lb 3 oz) white cabbage
1¼ tablespoons sea salt
1 teaspoon caraway seeds

Makes 1 × 1 litre (34 fl oz) jar

1 Remove the outer leaves of the cabbage, keeping them to pack the sauerkraut in its jar later on. Slice the cabbage on a mandoline (or use a sharp knife to get the slices really thin), and toss in a bowl.

2 Add the salt and scrunch and squeeze together with your hands for 15 minutes. At the end, you should have a pool of salty cabbage liquid. If there's enough liquid to cover your cabbage fully, you've done a good job squeezing.

3 When the cabbage starts to feel limp and releases water, mix in the caraway seeds. Start transferring it to a large, sterilised jar. Once you've filled up half of the jar, press it down hard with your hands to get rid of any air bubbles. Then add the rest, making sure to leave a few centimetres of air on the top. You want to ensure the cabbage is covered by its own liquid. Push the outer cabbage leaves on top to help keep the kraut submerged, pressing down hard to reduce any air bubbles, and then fill a zip-lock bag with water and put this on top, leaving the kraut tightly packed in the jar. Put on the lid.

4 Leave to rest at room temperature (away from direct sunlight) for 2 weeks. Test the kraut every few days until you like the flavour. If you prefer more tang, just leave it at room temperature a bit longer. When you're happy with it, transfer it to a smaller vessel or vessels and refrigerate. It will keep for 6 months in the fridge.

Kraut Variations

Here are a few suggestions for kraut, but you can get creative and just add whatever you like and see what works!

Ginger & Lemon Kraut
Add 1 grated carrot, a 3 cm (1¼ in) piece of ginger, grated, 1 tablespoon of black sesame seeds and the juice of half a lemon after the scrunching stage.

Jalapeño Kraut
Use red cabbage and add 2 sliced jalapeños after the scrunching stage.

KRAUT TIPS

1   If you don't have enough liquid to cover the cabbage, make a 2 per cent brine solution: 1 tablespoon of salt with 1 litre (34 fl oz) of water. Add as much as you need to submerge the kraut.

2   If any mould and gunk starts to form, just skim it off. The kraut will be fine, as it's preserved by the lactic acid.

3   Sit the jar on a small dish as the kraut can burp and leak over from the jar during the fermentation process.

From top to bottom: Proper Kraut (see page 60), Jalapeño Kraut (above), Ginger & Lemon Kraut (above)

KIMCHI

I remember the first ever time that I ate kimchi. It was on a flight to Sydney via Seoul, and it was served by the airline along with bibimbap, a classic Korean rice dish. My mind was blown; I'd never tasted anything like it: sweet, salty, sour, zingy, spicy – amazingness. I started experimenting with my own kimchi, looking to the *Momofuku* cookbook for inspiration from their signature Napa cabbage kimchi recipe.

For those that ask me what kimchi is, my answer tends to be 'It's like a Korean sauerkraut'. Really, it's a dish of fermented vegetables, and the most common version is with Napa cabbage. But you can really kimchi anything – Brussels sprout tops, radishes, kale, pear – just follow the seasons and experiment until you find your favourite combination.

You can eat kimchi straight from the jar or as a side dish, or use it as a cooking ingredient for things like F.A.T Kimchi Hot Sauce (see page 74), Kimchi Butter (see page 82), Kimchi Hollandaise (see page 79) and Kimchi & Stilton Grilled Sandwiches (see page 121).

From top to bottom: F.A.T Sesame Kimchi (see page 71), Daikon Kimchi (see page 66), Napa Kimchi (see page 68), Kale Kimchi (see page 69)

Daikon Kimchi

1 daikon (mooli) radish, cut
 into 1 cm (½ in) cubes
1 tablespoon sea salt, plus
 2 teaspoons
2 tablespoons granulated
 (raw) sugar
2 garlic cloves, peeled
 and crushed
1 thumb-sized piece fresh
 ginger, grated
3½ tablespoons gochugaru
 (Korean chilli powder)
2 tablespoons fish sauce

Makes 1 × 500 ml (17 fl oz) jar

1 Put the daikon in a large bowl and add 1 tablespoon of
   salt and 1 tablespoon of sugar. Toss well. Leave to stand
   for 20 minutes in a colander, set over a bowl.
2 Use your hands to squeeze out excess liquid from the
   daikon into your bowl of daikon juices, and set aside.
3 In another bowl, whisk together the remaining ingredients
   with 2 tablespoons of the reserved daikon juices. Now
   add the daikon and toss until well coated.
4 Put the daikon in a clean jar or plastic container, pressing
   it down well. Put the lid on and refrigerate. This will
   be ready to eat in 4 days.

This is a classic and
simple kimchi recipe.
Serve it cold for extra
crispness.

The most common type of kimchi is Napa kimchi. Some traditional recipes contain flour to act as a thickener, and here I use sweet rice flour.

Napa Cabbage Kimchi

2 large Chinese cabbages,
  600g–700g (1 lb 5 oz–
  1 lb 8 oz) each
130 g (4½ oz/1 cup) sea salt
45 g (1½ oz/¼ cup) sweet rice
  flour
50 g (2 oz/¼ cup) granulated
  (raw) sugar
1 carrot, grated
½ daikon (mooli) radish,
  grated
1 large thumb-sized piece
  fresh ginger, peeled and
  grated
1 medium onion, roughly
  chopped
10 garlic cloves, peeled
150 g (5 oz) gochugaru
  (Korean red chilli powder)
70 ml (2¼ fl oz) fish sauce
10 spring onions (scallions),
  roughly chopped

Makes 1½ kg (3 lb 4 oz)

1 Rinse the cabbage well and drain. Chuck out any damaged outer leaves. Slice the cabbage into quarters and discard the core.
2 Pour 5 litres (1½ gallons) of water in a large plastic container and add the salt. Stir until the salt dissolves. Add the cabbage and leave to stand, covered, overnight at room temperature.
3 Combine 750ml (25½ fl oz) of water, the rice flour and sugar in a large pan and bring to the boil. Reduce the heat to low and simmer for a few minutes, while stirring occasionally, until the mixture thickens. Take off the heat and allow to cool completely.
4 Drain the cabbage and chop into 2 cm (¾ in) strips. Put in a bowl with the grated carrot and daikon. Set aside.
5 In a food processor, blitz the ginger, onion, garlic, gochugaru and fish sauce. Put in a large bowl and fold in the flour slurry.
6 Put on disposable gloves. Add the cabbage mixture and spring onions and use your hands to combine well.
7 Transfer the kimchi to a clean, plastic container, cover and leave at room temperature for 24 hours. The kimchi will be ready to eat in 4–5 days and will be great at around 2 weeks. You can definitely eat it after that – as with all kimchis, it will get better with age. This will keep for up to a month.

Kale Kimchi

2 teaspoons sea salt
1 large bunch kale (approx.
  500 g/1 lb 2 oz), stems
  removed, chopped into
  1 cm (½ in) strips
1 carrot, grated
1 apple, grated
2 spring onions (scallions),
  finely chopped
50 g (2 oz/¼ cup) sweet rice
  flour
25 g (¾ oz/⅛ cup) granulated
  (raw) sugar
2 cm (1 in) piece fresh
  ginger, peeled and grated
4 garlic cloves, peeled
  and grated
1½ tablespoons gochugaru
  (Korean red chilli powder)
20 ml (¾ fl oz) fish sauce

Makes 600 g (1 lb 5 oz)

1 Put the salt and 250 ml (8½ fl oz) of water in a large bowl
   or plastic container, and stir until the salt has dissolved.
2 Add the kale to the salted water and mix well.
   Cover and let sit at room temperature overnight.
3 Drain the kale and and add the carrot, apple and
   spring onions.
4 Combine 125 ml (4 fl oz) of water, rice flour and sugar
   in a medium-sized pan and bring to the boil. Reduce
   the heat to low and simmer for a few minutes, while
   stirring occasionally, until the mixture thickens.
   Take off the heat and allow to cool completely.
5 Combine the ginger, garlic, gochugaru and fish sauce
   in a large bowl and then fold in the flour slurry.
6 Put on disposable gloves. Add the kale and use your
   hands to combine well.
7 Transfer the kimchi to a clean, plastic container, cover
   and leave at room temperature for 24 hours. The kimchi
   will be ready to eat in 3–4 days and lasts for up to 1 week.

A power food like kale,
fermented – this is like the
Gwyneth Paltrow of kimchi!

Often, seafood – in the shape of salted shrimp or fish sauces – is added to kick start the fermentation of kimchi. We, at F.A.T, developed this Napa cabbage kimchi for our events and pop-ups where we'd make kimchi quesadillas that people went nuts for. We never had much of an offering for veggies (except for a serving of house pickles, obvs) so we decided to omit the fishy elements like salted shrimp and fish sauce, and instead used sesame oil, sesame seeds and extra soy, which totally worked and bumps up the umami vibes even more.

F.A.T Sesame Kimchi

2 large Chinese cabbage
   600g–700g (1 lb 5 oz–
   1 lb 8 oz) each
2 tablespoons sea salt
100 g (3½ oz/½ cup)
   granulated (raw) sugar,
   plus 2 tablespoons
3½ tablespoons gochugaru
   (Korean red chilli powder)
3 garlic cloves, peeled and
   crushed or finely chopped
1 thumb-sized piece fresh
   ginger, peeled and grated
60 ml (2 fl oz) light soy sauce
50 ml (2 fl oz) sesame oil
5 spring onion stalks
   (scallions), finely chopped
3 tablespoons sesame seeds

Makes 1½ kg (3 lb 4 oz)

1　Rinse the cabbage well and drain. Chuck out any damaged outer leaves.
2　Slice the cabbage in half, then cut it into 4 pieces lengthways. Next, chop the cabbage into slices about 1 cm (½ in) thick.
3　Put the cabbage into a large plastic container and add the salt and 2 tablespoons sugar. Toss well, put the lid on the container and chill in the fridge for 24 hours.
4　Remove the cabbage from the fridge. (Ideally, you want to do this an hour before handling it to keep your hands from getting super cold.) Take handfuls of cabbage, and squeeze out as much of the liquid as you can.
5　In a separate bowl or plastic container, add the gochugaru, the remaining sugar, garlic and ginger and mix well. Add water if it's too thick, then stir in the soy sauce and sesame oil.
6　If you're scared of garlicky fingers, wear disposable gloves. Add the cabbage, spring onion and sesame seeds to the slurry and use your hands to mix really well, squeezing the paste into the cabbage.
7　Return the cabbage to the large plastic container, put on the lid and refrigerate. The kimchi will taste nice within 1 week, and start to build up a nice funk after 2 weeks. After those 2 weeks you can keep fermenting it as it will just get fizzier and funkier. This will keep for up to 1 month.

SAUCES

'You know what they put on French fries in Holland instead of ketchup?'

'What?'

'Mayonnaise.'

'Mayonnaise?'

'I seen 'em do it, man, they f*ckin' drown 'em in that shit!'

– Vincent Vega and Jules Winnfield, *Pulp Fiction*

I'm Dutch, and yes, I put sauce on everything. A friend once told me that Dutch people use fries simply as vessels to consume as as much sauce as possible. I don't think there's anything wrong with that.

Inspired by my favourite chilli sauces like sriracha and the LA/Mexico hybrid Tapatío, this kimchi hot sauce is a blend of F.A.T Sesame Kimchi (see page 71) with a charred and smoky chilli sauce. It takes forever to make and it takes forever to ferment, so you need quite a bit of patience. But then once you've made it, you know you'll want to put this on everything. And you'll go nuts if you ever run out. As one of my stockists, Ebony Harding, who runs London's lovely Harringay Local Store, put it, 'I've just run out of hot sauce and I don't know if I can eat Scotch eggs without it!' Eat with scrambled eggs, pork buns, tacos, fried chicken, pizza – anything goes.

F.A.T Kimchi Hot Sauce

250 g (9 oz) F.A.T
Sesame Kimchi (see page 71)

for the red hot sauce:
500 g (1 lb 2 oz) hot red chillies
(I use a mix of red
jalapeños, habaneros and
any other red chillies I can
get my hands on)
2 white onions, peeled
2 garlic cloves, peeled
2 teaspoons vegetable oil
1 teaspoon sea salt, plus extra
to taste
500 ml (17 fl oz) rice wine
vinegar
125 ml (4 fl oz) honey

Makes 2 × 250 ml (8½ fl oz) jars

Red hot sauce
1 Preheat your oven to 180°C (350°F/Gas 4).
2 Put on your disposable gloves. Rinse the chillies thoroughly, and remove all the stalks. Remember, these things are hot and your eyes (or other body parts) don't like them.
3 Put half the quantity of chillies in a roasting tray with 1 onion and 1 garlic clove. Roast for 40 minutes, until the chillies are charred.
4 Meanwhile, dice the remaining chillies, onion and garlic and fry with the oil and salt in a heavy-based pan over a medium to high heat for 5 minutes. Pour in 750 ml (25 fl oz) of water and cook for another 60 minutes, until the chillies have softened. Take off the heat and allow to cool.
5 Remove the chillies, onion and garlic from the oven, and let them come to room temperature.
6 Put both chilli mixtures in a food processor and blitz, slowly adding in the vinegar and honey, until you have a smooth consistency.
7 Transfer to a clean, plastic container, cover and refrigerate. Once fully chilled, taste and season the hot sauce with more salt or honey if it needs it. Refrigerate for 2 weeks before using.

Kimchi hot sauce
1 Make sure your kimchi and hot sauce have aged for at least 2 weeks. Once ready, blend the kimchi to a purée.
2 In a large mixing bowl, combine the kimchi purée with your red hot sauce. Blend well.
3 You can now bottle or jar your sauce in a sterilised jar or bottle. Keep in the fridge and eat within 2 weeks.

It's natural for the kimchi hot sauce to keep fermenting, so minimise this by keeping it in the fridge.

F·A·T

LONDON

KIMCHI HOT SAUCE

made in clapton

We all know and love Heinz tomato ketchup. What you might not know is that ketchup was born in Asia under the names *kecap* and *ketjap* and began life as a fermented fish sauce. The sauce was transported to Europe by Dutch traders and was then developed into different condiments including mushroom ketchup and, eventually, tomato ketchup. If you're all about that fifth flavour, though, try this recipe with anchovies, mushrooms and soy – they add a lot of extra power to an already umami-rich tomato blend.

Umami Ketchup

3 tablespoons olive oil
1 white onion, chopped
2 × 400 g (14 oz) tinned
  tomatoes
1½ tablespoons tomato purée
125 ml (4 fl oz) cider vinegar
90 g (3 oz / ⅓ cup) dark brown
  sugar
1 teaspoon sea salt
pinch chilli flakes
3 anchovies in oil, drained
2 teaspoons light soy sauce
2 tablespoons mushroom
  powder
1 teaspoon oyster sauce
2 teaspoons Worcestershire
  sauce
sea salt and freshly ground
  black pepper

Makes 4 × 300 ml (10 fl oz)
  jars

1 Heat the olive oil in a large pan and add the onions. Cook over a low heat, for 20 minutes, until softened.
2 Meanwhile, in a food processor, purée the tinned tomatoes. Add them to the onion and cook over a low heat for 15 minutes.
3 Add the tomato purée, vinegar, sugar, salt and chilli, and continue to cook on a low heat for another hour.
4 Add the anchovies, soy sauce, mushroom powder, oyster and Worcestershire sauces. Take the pan off the heat and allow to cool completely. Blitz to make the ketchup as smooth as possible. Taste and season.
5 Decant into sterilised glass bottles or jars, seal, allow to cool and refrigerate for up to 2 weeks. It will be ready to eat immediately once chilled, but the flavours will intensify after a few days – I find it at its best after 4–5 days.

This is inspired by the famous chilli oil from China that you can find in Asian shops worldwide, with the grandma on it (*Lao Gan Ma*: 'Old Godmother'), which is basically the godmother of all chilli oils. I figured that this amazing condiment would probably taste even better if made at home, from scratch, and I added a few Mexican chillies picked up from my travels along the way. And it's gooooood! Add this chilli oil to rice, ramen, or any Asian dish looking for a bit of a kick. It's my go-to sauce for mixing with black vinegar when eating dumplings at home, and it's especially great as a base for my favourite comfort dish of all time, Dan Dan Noodles (see page 100).

Szechuan Chilli Oil

2 tablespoons cumin seeds
175 g (6 oz) Szechuan
   peppercorns
150 g (5 oz) fermented black
   beans, coarsely chopped
3 tablespoons crushed garlic
100 g (3½ oz) gochugaru
   (Korean chilli powder)
500 ml (17 fl oz) sunflower oil
4 shallots, finely chopped
1 thumb-sized piece fresh
   ginger, grated
250 ml (8½ fl oz) sesame oil
100 g (3½ oz) dried chillies
   (chile de arbol, aguajillo,
   chipotle or dried hot red
   chilli of your choice)
220 g (8 oz/1 cup) granulated
   (raw) sugar
1 teaspoon sea salt

Makes 4 × 300 ml jars
   (10 fl oz) jars

1 In a dry pan, toast the cumin seeds and Szechuan peppercorns over low heat until aromatic. Remove from the heat and grind in a pestle and mortar, or a coffee or spice grinder, until fine.

2 Put the fermented black beans, garlic, chilli powder, ground cumin and Szechuan peppercorns in a warmed sterilised jar (in this order).

3 Add the sunflower oil to a pan and heat over medium to high heat until small bubbles start to form – but do not let it boil. Add the shallots and ginger and fry until just crispy and golden brown. Immediately remove from the heat (you want to make sure they don't burn) and pour the hot oil, ginger and shallots over the spices and black beans in the jar. Stir.

4 Using the same pan, add the sesame oil and set over medium to high heat until hot. Add the dried chillies and cook for 10 minutes until softened.

5 Add the sugar and salt to the pan and stir until completely dissolved. Take off the heat and allow to cool briefly.

6 Once cool enough to handle, transfer the chillies to a food processor or blender and process until you have a paste. Add to the jar and give everything a quick stir. Cover and allow to cool completely. The chilli oil will be ready to eat in 3–4 days and will last for 6 months. There's no need to refrigerate this.

Relax. Everything so far has been pretty straightforward in this book. They're essentially a bunch of recipes that you can't f*ck up. The thought of making hollandaise can freak people out, and yes, I've made numerous curdled, split sauces in my life. So if it doesn't work, try it again. It'll be worth it. Serve for breakfast with eggs Benedict.

Kimchi Hollandaise

1 tablespoon F.A.T
*   Sesame Kimchi (see page 71)*
2 medium egg yolks
pinch of sea salt
pinch of gochugaru
*   (Korean red chilli powder)*
125 g (4 oz) unsalted
*   butter, melted*
lemon juice or white wine
*   vinegar (optional)*

Makes 4 servings

1 Blitz the F.A.T Sesame Kimchi with 1 tablespoon of its liquid in a food processor until it is as smooth as possible. Press through a sieve into a bowl so you end up with a smooth, thin sauce.
2 Put the egg yolks in a heatproof bowl and place on top of a saucepan of simmering water. Make sure the bowl doesn't touch the water.
3 Add the kimchi sauce, a pinch of sea salt and the gochugaru chilli powder and whisk.
4 Over a low heat, slowly mix in the melted butter, bit by bit, whisking thoroughly. You should end up with a smooth, thick sauce. You can loosen it with some lemon juice or white vine vinegar if it needs it. If the mixture begins to split, add an ice cube and whisk briskly.
5 Serve immediately. You've done it! (Hopefully.)

I think of this as a jazzed-up, cheesy ranch dressing. It is excellent with pickles, especially with the Pickled Nashi Pear (see page 31), Sweet Fennel Pickles (see page 31), Bourbon Pickled Okra (see page 32), Cucumber Dill Pickles (see page 17), Orange Blossom Carrots (see page 43) and Rose Radishes (see page 43).

Stilton Dip

200 ml (7 fl oz) buttermilk
100 g (3½ oz) Stilton or
*   similar blue cheese,*
*   crumbled*
200 ml (7 fl oz) soured cream
1 teaspoon mayonnaise
1 teaspoon tahini
4 tablespoons pickle of
*   choice, very finely chopped*
*   (Bourbon Pickled Okra*
*   on page 32 and Pickled*
*   Jalapeños on page 119 are*
*   both good options)*
1 tablespoon lemon juice
dash of DIY Sriracha
*   (see page 86)*
sea salt and freshly ground
*   black pepper, to taste*
olive oil, to drizzle
chives, to garnish
sesame seeds, to garnish

Makes 300 ml (10 fl oz)

1 Put all the ingredients except the olive oil, chives and sesame seeds in a bowl and whisk together until smooth.
2 Taste and check for seasoning.
3 Drizzle with olive oil, and top with chives and sesame seeds.

Kimchi butter. OK, technically not a sauce, but it's amazing if you smear it onto grilled corn on the cob or steak, or use it instead of plain butter when making scrambled eggs. I find slathering it onto warm, toasted Turkish bread and serving it with some pickles and a beer works pretty damn fine, too.

Kimchi Butter

4 tablespoons F.A.T Sesame Kimchi (see page 71)
90 g (3 oz) salted butter, at room temperature
½ tablespoon white miso paste

Makes 100 g (3½ oz)

1 Blitz the F.A.T Sesame Kimchi into a purée using a food processor.
2 You want to draw out most of the moisture of the kimchi here, so place it in muslin (cheesecloth) and squeeze out all the liquid.
3 Whisk the butter until it starts to get fluffy, then whisk in the miso paste and kimchi until thoroughly combined and airy.
4 Transfer the butter to a plastic container, or wrap it in cling film (plastic wrap) and shape into a log.
5 Refrigerate for 1 hour before using. The butter will keep in the fridge for up to 1 week.

Pickled seeds are a great way to add some texture and zing to dishes. Serve them on a charcuterie board, with a pork pie or a pastrami sandwich. They sort of pop in your mouth like caviar!

Pickled Mustard Seeds

7 tablespoons yellow mustard seeds
250 ml (8½ fl oz) cider vinegar
4 tablespoons granulated (raw) sugar
2 tablespoons sea salt

Makes 1 × 300 ml (10 fl oz) jar

1 Toast the mustard seeds in a dry medium-sized skillet until fragrant. Remove and set aside to cool.
2 Combine the vinegar, sugar, salt and 125 ml (4 fl oz) of water in a pan and bring to a boil over high heat. Turn the heat to low and add the mustard seeds. Simmer for 1 hour, until the seeds start to plump up as they absorb the liquid. If too much liquid evaporates, just add some more water to cover the seeds.
3 Take off the heat. Let the mixture come to room temperature, transfer to a clean jar or plastic container, cover and refrigerate. Your pickled mustard seeds will be ready to use in 3 days and keep for up 1 month in the fridge.

There's an Italian, jam-like condiment called *Mostarda di frutta*, which is made of candied fruits and mustard essence. This is my savoury interpretation of that dish – a sweet fruity but spicy mustard. Serve it with sausages, ham hock, or anything else you'd normally put store-bought mustard on really!

Plum Mustard

4½ tablespoons Pickled Mustard Seeds (see above), strained
2 tablespoons cider vinegar
3 teaspoons English mustard powder
50 g (2 oz/¼ cup) granulated (raw) sugar
5 Cardamom Pickled Greengages (page 36), skins on
pinch of sea salt

Makes 1 × 300 ml (10 fl oz) jar

1 Blitz the pickled mustard seeds and vinegar in a food processer until smooth.
2 With the motor still running, add the mustard powder, sugar and the flesh from the pickled greengages.
3 Scrape down the sides of the food processor and blitz again, slowly adding 1 tablespoon of hot water.
4 Check for seasoning and thickness, add salt and a little more water if you think it needs it. Remember: you're going for the consistency of mustard.
5 Pour the mustard into a clean jar or plastic container, put on the lid and refrigerate. The mustard can be eaten straight away or you can keep it for up to 1 week in the fridge.

I know what you think. Why on earth would you make your own sriracha sauce if you can just buy the awesome version from Huy Fong Foods, a company many consider to be the OG sriracha makers? Well, the answer is simple. Because it's really easy and totally delicious. Also, remember the sriracha crisis when it was rumoured that the infamous Huy Fong Foods factory was closing down, which caused hot sauce nerds to go all *28 Days Later*, buying up sriracha all over the world in case they would never be able to find it again? Well, just in case that drama happens again, here's how to make your own.

DIY Sriracha

500 g (1 lb 2 oz) red jalapeños
200 g (7 oz) red Thai chillies
100 g (3½ oz) red Scotch
  bonnet chillies
6 garlic cloves, peeled
45 g (1¾ oz / ¼ cup) light
  brown sugar
1 tablespoon sea salt
125 ml (4 fl oz) rice wine
  vinegar

Makes 1 × 300 ml (10 fl oz)
  jar or bottle

1 Put on your disposable gloves. Rinse the chillies thoroughly, and remove all the stalks. Remember, these things are hot and your eyes (and other body parts) don't like them.
2 Put the chillies in a food processor with the garlic, brown sugar, salt and 125 ml (4 fl oz) of water. Blitz until smooth.
3 Transfer the mixture to a clean jar and cover it with muslin (cheesecloth). Secure with butcher's string. Put the jar on a plate in case the mixture 'burps' and overflows. Leave to ferment at room temperature for 5 days.
4 Pour the fermented chilli mixture into the food processor and add the vinegar. Blitz until smooth.
5 Put the mixture through a fine mesh strainer into a pan, using the back of a spoon to push it through. You want to remove all the pulp and seeds so you end up with a super-smooth sauce. It will be a fairly thin sauce at this stage. Reserve the pulp to make your own chilli oil (see tip below).
6 Bring the hot sauce to the boil over a medium to high heat. Reduce the heat to low and simmer for 30 minutes, until the sauce has reduced to your preferred thickness. If foam appears on top of the sauce, just use a spoon to carefully skim it off.
7 Take off the heat and leave the sriracha to cool to room temperature before bottling and refrigerating. Congrats, you've made your own sriracha! It should keep for a few months.

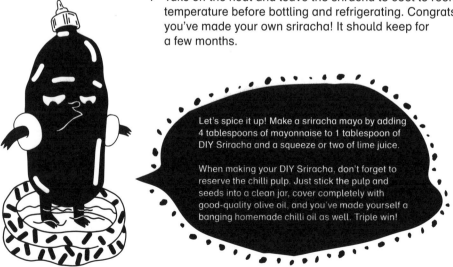

Let's spice it up! Make a sriracha mayo by adding 4 tablespoons of mayonnaise to 1 tablespoon of DIY Sriracha and a squeeze or two of lime juice.

When making your DIY Sriracha, don't forget to reserve the chilli pulp. Just stick the pulp and seeds into a clean jar, cover completely with good-quality olive oil, and you've made yourself a banging homemade chilli oil as well. Triple win!

THE RECIPES

Now you have lots of jars of pickles, sauces and kimchis in your fridge, you'll want to know how to eat them – right? So here are some of my favourite sandwich, taco and noodle recipes that incorporate all the tasty things you now know how to make.

I also asked a few of my food friends and fellow pickle lovers if they could share their personal faves.

You're now ready to throw your own #pickleparty!

Dutch people go mad when the season's first new herring arrive. They start to appear in May or June, and they are literally at every street corner stand and market. If you want to get real authentic when eating this, lift a herring by its tail, dip it in the raw onion, hold it above your head, then throw your neck back and lower it into your mouth.

Dutch New Herring

4 whole herrings (ask your fishmonger to remove the heads, scale the fish and remove the roe)
sea salt (enough to cover your herring)
¼ white onion, finely sliced
handful of Amsterdam Onions (see below)

Makes enough for 4

1 Freeze the herring for 24 hours. This will kill any bacteria in the flesh.
2 The next day, rinse the herring under cold water and pat dry with paper towels.
3 Put into a clean container and sprinkle each herring with the salt, making sure they are completely covered.
4 Cover and refrigerate for at least 24 hours and up to 3–4 days.
5 The herring will have softened by now. Rinse well under cold water, then soak in a bowl of fresh cold water for 8 hours. You need to refresh the water every now and then.
6 Once ready to eat, fillet the fish and remove the bones.
7 Serve the herring with the white onion sprinkled on top and the Amsterdam Onions. This will keep for 2 days.

I already told you that the word pickle comes from the Dutch word *pekel*, which means brine. So it's no surprise that pickles are a big part of my motherland and my upbringing. These bright yellow pickled onions were my favourite as a kid. You'd see huge jars of them in the back of the *frituur*, which is like our Dutch version of a fish 'n' chip shop or a dirty kebab place.

Amsterdam Onions

250 g (9 oz) pickling onions
250 ml (8½ fl oz) white wine
250 ml (8½ fl oz) cider vinegar
6 saffron threads
1 bay leaf
1 teaspoon mustard seeds
2 tablespoons granulated (raw) sugar
pinch of sea salt

Makes 1 × 500 ml (17 fl oz) jar

1 Place the onions in a large bowl and cover in boiling water. Leave for 1 minute, then drain and allow to cool.
2 Once cool enough to handle, peel the onions and pop them into a clean jar.
3 Combine the vinegars, and remaining ingredients in a medium-sized pan and bring to the boil.
4 Take off the heat and immediately pour the hot vinegar-brine over the onions in the jar.
5 Allow to cool, put the lid on and refrigerate for 3 weeks before eating. These will keep in the fridge for 6 months.

Taiwanese street food heroes BAO have come a long way since they started in 2012 at Kerb, one of London's original and best street food market initiatives. After doing the market rounds they quickly opened a semi-permanent site at Hackney's Netil Market, and in 2015 they opened up a proper bricks-and-mortar restaurant. They serve inventive Taiwanese small plates, and of course baos with a couple of different fillings. Their signature dish? The *gua bao*: a fluffy white steamed bun, topped with braised pork, peanut powder, coriander and fermented mustard greens. It's the real deal – you won't find store-bought hoisin sauce anywhere near these guys.

I'm massively impressed, not only with what I think is some of the most interesting, creative and tasty food in London, but also with what they've managed to achieve in such a short amount of time. Go team BAO. Here's their recipe for soy pickled chillies, which are delicious spooned over freshly shucked oysters.

Soy Pickled Chillies with Oysters

by the team from BAO London

6 tablespoons rice wine
  vinegar
120ml (4 fl oz)
  Chinkiang vinegar
  (black rice vinegar)
2 tablespoons light soy sauce
12 garlic cloves, peeled and
  very finely chopped
½ tablespoon sea salt
1 tablespoon granulated
  (raw) sugar
12 green jalapeños
fresh oysters, cleaned,
  to serve

Makes 1 × 300 ml (10 fl oz) jar

1 In a saucepan over low heat, combine the vinegars, soy sauce, garlic, salt and sugar. Stir until the salt and sugar have dissolved.
2 Slice the jalapeños in half lengthways, remove and discard the seeds, and chop finely.
3 Add the jalapeños to the vinegar-brine. Pour into a clean jar, put the lid on and set aside to pickle overnight.
4 The next day your soy pickled chillies are ready to eat. Spoon the pickles and their brine over freshly shucked oysters.
5 If kept in the refrigerator, the pickled chillies will last for 1 month.

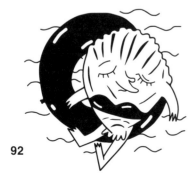

These babies taste pretty good and boozy as plain old pickles, but they're next level if you fry them. Because everything tastes better when you fry it, right? I love to serve these with my Smoky Crema Dip (see below), but they are also great with Kimchi Hot Sauce (see page 74) or Stilton Dip (see page 81). Snack on these while doing Picklebacks (see page 129).

Bourbon & Chilli Okra Fries

200 g (7 oz) Bourbon Pickled
  Okra (see page 32)
125 g (4 oz/1 cup) plain
  (all-purpose) flour
300 ml (10 fl oz) beer
1 medium egg, beaten
¼ teaspoon sea salt
¼ teaspoon freshly ground
  black pepper
vegetable oil
Smoky Crema Dip, to serve

Makes enough for 2–4

1 Take the okra out of its brine and place on some paper towels to get rid of any excess liquid before frying.
2 Put the flour, beer, egg, salt and pepper in a zip-lock bag and shake until well mixed. Add the okra, and shake until the okra is coated in the flour mixture.
3 Heat the oil to 180°C (350°F), testing for the right temperature with a thermometer. Line a surface with newspapers or paper towels.
4 Carefully add the okra and fry in batches for about 2 minutes, until golden brown. Transfer the okra to the paper towels or newspapers to drain. Serve immediately with a dip.

Smoky Crema Dip
Make an awesome, smoky dip by roasting 10 spring onions (scallions) in a hot oven until they're properly charred – don't use any oil when doing this. Blitz them in a food processor with a good glug of olive oil, a handful of fresh coriander (cilantro) and 1 garlic clove. Pop it in a bowl and stir through 200 ml (7 fl oz) of soured cream, 1 tablespoon of mayonnaise and fresh lime juice, to taste. Season with salt and pepper.

This really is the ultimate meatball sandwich: juicy pork and fennel meatballs, a rich tomato sauce, crunchy sweet fennel pickles and a nutty, dreamy pesto. My meatballs and tomato sauce are adapted from recipes in *The Frankies Spuntino Kitchen Companion & Cooking Manual*, the must-have cookbook from the two chefs behind the popular NYC Frankies Spuntino restaurants.

The Ultimate Meatball Sandwich

butter, to spread
4 slices of good-quality
* sourdough bread*
olive oil, to grease
Walnut & Rocket Pesto
* (see page 98)*
2 good handfuls of Sweet
* Fennel Pickles (around*
* ½ cup) (see page 31)*

for the tomato sauce:
125 ml (4 fl oz) olive oil
5 garlic cloves, peeled and
* finely chopped*
2 × 400 g (14 oz) tinned
* tomatoes, chopped roughly*
* or crushed with your hands*
1 teaspoon sea salt

for the meatballs:
500 g (1 lb 2 oz) minced
* (ground) pork*
1 tablespoon fennel seeds,
* toasted*
2 garlic cloves, finely chopped
1 medium egg
1 teaspoon sea salt
1 teaspoon freshly ground
* black pepper*
2 tablespoons chopped
* raisins*
2 tablespoons grated
* Parmesan*
1 slice of white bread, torn
* into very small pieces*

Makes enough for 2

1 To make the tomato sauce, heat the oil in a pan and add the garlic. Cook over medium heat for a few minutes until the garlic is fragrant and golden.
2 Add the tomatoes and their juices along with the salt. Simmer for 3–4 hours, stirring occasionally.
3 About an hour before your sauce is ready, make the meatballs. Combine the ingredients in a bowl until well mixed.
4 Preheat the oven to 180°C (350°F/Gas 4).
5 Form the meatball mixture into golf ball-sized portions. Pat them down slightly and place them on a tray lined with baking paper.
6 Bake in the oven for 20 minutes, until browned.
7 Remove the meatballs from the oven and put them in the tomato sauce. Simmer the meatballs in the sauce for around 20 minutes, until cooked through.
8 To make the sandwich, spread the butter on one side of each slice of bread, and don't be shy. If using a toastie maker, put 2 slices of bread, butter side facing down, on to the grill. If you don't have a toastie maker, heat a large, heavy-based pan over medium heat and add a tiny dash of oil. Put 2 slices of bread, butter side facing down, in the pan.
9 Now add the toppings in this order, making sure every inch of your bread is covered with something tasty: Walnut & Rocket Pesto, Sweet Fennel Pickles, meatballs and 2 extra spoonfuls of tomato sauce. Top the sandwiches with your remaining slices of bread, butter side facing up. If using a toastie maker, press down hard so things don't start falling out, and toast until done.
10 If using a pan, put a sheet of foil or baking paper on top of the sandwiches followed by a casserole dish (the weight of the dish will press the sandwich down). Fry over medium to low heat, until golden on one side, then flip over and repeat with the other side. Serve while still hot.

This pesto is a great, nuttier and cheaper alternative to your regular basil one. It is super in the Ultimate Meatball Sandwich on page 97.

Walnut & Rocket Pesto

100 g (3½ oz) rocket
  (arugula), washed
  and roughly chopped
2 garlic cloves, peeled
small handful of walnuts
small handful of grated
  Parmesan
juice of 1 lemon
extra virgin olive oil,
  as needed
sea salt and freshly ground
  black pepper, to taste

Makes 1 x 190 ml (7 fl oz) jar

1 Put the rocket, garlic, walnuts, Parmesan and lemon juice in a blender or food processor. Blitz to get a rough paste, then add the oil gradually until you've reached your preferred consistency. I like it to be quite thick, especially if using in the Ultimate Meatball Sandwich, just to minimise any bits dribbling onto your shirt!
2 Season to taste, then pour into a clean jar. Store in the fridge until ready to use. Ensure that the jar is airtight and the pesto is kept covered with oil and it will keep in the fridge for 2 months.

In 2013, I hosted the UK premiere for *The Great Chicken Wing Hunt*, a documentary about a group of people in the US that go on a mission to find the world's best Buffalo wing. The event raised money for the charity FoodCycle by asking for a small entrance fee. In return, guests received unlimited beers and a plethora of chicken wings. I asked some of my favourite food people, such as BAO, The Skinny Bib, Tomos Parry, Rita's and On The Bab, to create a hot sauce. We trimmed 1000 chicken wings, fried them and covered them in everyone's different sauces. Here is our F.A.T version from that night. It's like a greedy all-in-one Buffalo wing, where the obligatory blue cheese dressing and celery stick are already in the sauce, so you can just scoff it up all at once!

F.A.T Buffalo Wings

vegetable oil, for deep-frying
12 chicken wings, trimmed,
 cut in half by the joint
90 g (3 oz) unsalted butter
125 ml (4 fl oz) F.A.T
 Kimchi Hot Sauce (page 74)
1 tablespoon Stilton or similar
 blue cheese
celery salt, to taste

Makes enough for 2–4

1 Fill a deep fryer or large, heavy-based pan with vegetable oil and heat to 190°C (375°F).
2 Carefully add the chicken wings, in batches, and fry for about 10 minutes until they're crispy and golden. Use a slotted spoon or tongs to remove the wings from the oil and drain on paper towels.
3 Melt the butter in a separate pan over low heat. Add the hot sauce and Stilton and celery salt, then stir until well combined and heated through.
4 Place the wings in a bowl, pour over the sauce, and toss. Serve straight away.

This is the dish I've probably made most in recent years: Dan Dan Noodles. It's my ultimate comfort food. Think of it like an AZN version of a spag bol (hence the name): essentially, Asian noodles with meat ragu. There are loads of variations on the dish, and this has become my favourite.

Dan Dan Noodles

400 g (14 oz) fresh udon noodles
100 g (3½ oz) Chinese greens
    (like bok choi or choi sum)
a handful of peanuts, roasted
    and chopped
2 spring onions (scallions),
    finely chopped
1 tablespoon black or white
    sesame seeds, toasted

for the pork:
1 tablespoon vegetable oil
5 cm (2 in) fresh ginger, peeled
    and finely chopped
4 garlic cloves, peeled and
    finely chopped
100 g (3½ oz) Pickled
    Mustard Greens (see
    page 53), chopped
250 g (9 oz) minced pork
1 teaspoon hoisin sauce
1 teaspoon five-spice powder
¼ teaspoon mushroom powder
2 tablespoons light soy sauce
1 tablespoon Shaoxing wine

for the sauce:
3 tablespoons tahini
1 tablespoon peanut butter
2 tablespoons Szechuan
    pepper, toasted and ground
1 teaspoon black Chinese
    vinegar
200 ml (7 fl oz) Szechuan
    Chilli Oil (see page 78)
2 tablespoons dark soy sauce
1 tablespoon granulated (raw)
    sugar
sea salt, to taste

Makes enough for 2

1   To make the pork, heat the oil in a large pan over medium-high heat. Add the ginger, garlic and Pickled Mustard Greens and stir-fry for a few minutes, until soft and fragrant.
2   Add the pork, using a spoon to break it up into chunks, then brown until the meat is a little crisp.
3   Add the hoisin sauce, five-spice and mushroom powders, soy sauce and Shaoxing wine, and stir through really well. Cook for another few minutes, until most of the liquid has evaporated. Set aside.
4   Cook the noodles according to the packet instructions. Scoop out about 200 ml (7 fl oz) of the cooking water, then drain the noodles, running them under cold water to stop them from cooking. Set aside.
5   To make the sauce, combine the tahini, peanut butter, Szechuan pepper, vinegar, Szechuan Chilli Oil, soy sauce, sugar and salt in a bowl. Stir through the reserved noodle cooking water until you have a saucy consistency. Check for seasoning.
6   Bring a large saucepan of water to the boil and blanch the Chinese greens for 2 minutes, over a medium heat. Drain when cooked and set aside.
7   To serve, divide the sauce between two bowls, add the noodles and give them a good stir so they're well coated in the sauce. Top with the pork with the blanched greens, peanuts, spring onions and sesame seeds. Stir through and eat!

The Chinese name 'dan dan' refers to the over-the-shoulder carrying poles with hanging baskets, that street vendors use – the noodles on one side, sauces on the other.

I've had a long-time love affair with chicken wings. As a kid, going to Gauchos restaurant in my hometown Maastricht with my dad and sister Eva was a massive treat – like, a way bigger treat than getting a McDonald's Happy Meal toy! These are kind of my grown-up version of those joyful kids' meals. The pickle juice, sugar, salt and spice-spiked brine helps the chicken stay juicy, and the buttermilk-flour coating provides a welcome crunch. Serve it with plenty of hot sauce and the obligatory side dish of pickles.

Pickle Fried Chicken Wings

12 chicken wings
300–500 ml (10–17 fl oz)
*   chilled cucumber dill pickle*
*   brine, strained and spices*
*   discarded*
vegetable oil, for deep-frying
500 ml (17 fl oz) buttermilk
300 g (10½ oz/2 cups) plain
*   (all-purpose) flour*
1 teaspoon sea salt, plus extra
*   to sprinkle*
black and white sesame
*   seeds, to sprinkle*
DIY Sriracha (see page 86),
*   to serve*

Makes enough for 2–4

1 Trim off the tips from the chicken wings and discard. Put the wings in a shallow bowl and add the brine, making sure the wings are completely submerged. Refrigerate and leave for at least 4 hours or, ideally, overnight to brine.
2 When you're ready to fry your wings, fill a deep fryer or large, heavy-based pan with the oil and heat to 190°C (375°F).
3 Grab 2 shallow bowls and fill one with the buttermilk, the other one with flour and salt mixed in.
4 One by one, dredge the wings in the buttermilk bowl followed by the flour.
5 Carefully add the wings to the hot oil and fry them, in batches, for about 10 minutes or until they're crispy and golden.
6 Use a slotted spoon or tongs to remove the wings from the oil and drain on paper towels. Sprinkle with sea salt and sesame seeds and serve with some DIY Srirarcha.

Because proper homemade flatbreads with offal and pickles are banging! A massive thanks to James Lowe for sharing his sourdough flatbread recipe.

Sourdough Flatbread with Cumin Lamb & Kebab Chillies

2 tablespoons plain yoghurt
1 tablespoons lemon juice
sea salt and freshly ground
    black pepper
Pickled Kebab Chillies, finely
    chopped (see page 35)
coriander (cilantro), leaves
    finely chopped

for the flatbread:
660 g (1 lb 7 oz/5½ cups)
    plain (all-purpose) flour,
    plus extra to dust
165 g (6 oz/1½ cups)
    spelt flour
4 teaspoons sea salt
125 g (4 oz/½ cup)
    soured cream
165 g (6 oz) sourdough starter

for the cumin lamb hearts:
2 lamb hearts, excess fat,
    tubes, gristle and coarse
    sinews removed (ask your
    butcher to do this)
1 tablespoon cumin seeds,
    toasted and ground
1 tablespoon Szechuan
    peppercorns, toasted and
    ground
olive oil
sea salt and freshly ground
    black pepper, to taste

Makes enough for 6

1 Make the sourdough flatbread. In a large bowl, combine the ingredients for the dough with 300 ml (10 fl oz) of water and mix with your hands for 5 minutes. Allow to rest for 1 hour.
2 Knead the dough on a lightly floured surface for 15–20 minutes then leave to rest for 3–4 hours, kneading and folding it every hour, until the texture is shiny and satiny.
3 Gather the dough into a ball and divide into 6 golf ball-sized rounds. Freeze any leftover dough.
4 Use floured hands to press each ball of dough flat and stretch out into 10 cm (4 in) rounds about 3 mm (⅛ in) thick. You could use a dusted rolling pin here.
5 To cook the flatbreads, heat a large, dry pan over a very high heat. Add the flatbread, cooking one at a time, and fry for 1 minute, until bubbles start to form on the top. Then, flip the bread and cook it for another minute. Take off the heat and wrap in foil to keep warm.
6 Rinse the hearts thoroughly in cold water and pat dry with paper towels. Cut each piece into 3 and put in a bowl with a good glug of olive oil and the ground spices. Season with salt and pepper and mix well.
7 Heat a heavy-based griddle or pan over high heat. When hot, add the hearts and brown all over.
8 In a small bowl, combine the yoghurt and lemon juice and season with salt and pepper.
9 To serve, top the flatbread with the yoghurt. Add the griddled hearts, a good spoonful of chopped pickles and a sprinkling of the coriander.

Sourdough Starter
To make the starter, all you need is water and some plain (all-purpose) flour. Pour 200 g (7 oz/1⅔ cups) of flour into a large, clean bowl or jar. Add 200 ml (7 fl oz) of water, mix well and cover with a kitchen towel. Put the bowl somewhere warm and leave overnight. The next day, you should start to see bubbles forming and the mixture beginning to swell. The bubbles mean that wild yeast have started to make themselves at home in your starter, and that it is ready for feeding. Feed your starter with equal amounts of flour and water for the next 3 days – your starter should be ready to use after about 5 days.

A recipe from James Lowe, head chef and owner of Lyle's, the modern, Michelin-starred British restaurant in east London. I look after the restaurant's marketing so needless to say, I'm a huge fan. The idea of this bun recipe comes from a combination of street food events James did in London, way before he opened his restaurant. As James explains, 'This is definitely not a typical Lyle's dish. It's just a fun combination of things I like that can be made quickly and simply, even for hundreds of people if you were so inclined! Underripe green tomatoes have an amazing, firm texture that stands up so well to pickling.'

Green Tomato, Mustard & Pork Belly Bun

by James Lowe, Head Chef & Owner of Lyle's

500 g (1 lb 2 oz) skinned bone-in pork belly
sea salt, to taste
5 sprigs of lemon thyme leaves
2 garlic cloves, peeled and crushed
4 brioche buns
50 g (2 oz) crispy shallots (buy these ready-made at Asian supermarkets)
1 butterhead lettuce, 4 leaves removed

for the pickled green tomatoes:
6 green tomatoes, cut into 5 mm (¼ in) slices
300 ml (10 fl oz) cider vinegar
1 teaspoon sea salt
150 g (5 oz/⅔ cup) granulated (raw) sugar
1 tablespoon cumin seeds
pinch of turmeric
1 white onion, thinly sliced

for the mustard mayonnaise:
1 medium egg, plus 2 egg yolks
1 tablespoon Dijon mustard
300 ml (10 fl oz) mild olive oil
wholegrain mustard, to taste
3 teaspoons cider vinegar
sea salt and freshly ground black pepper

Makes enough for 4

1 Make the pickled green tomatoes the day before you want to eat this. Put the ingredients for the tomatoes and 250 ml (8½ fl oz) water in a heavy-based pan and bring to the boil.
2 Remove the tomatoes from the pan and place in a clean jar. Reserve the liquid and allow to cool to 60°C (140°F).
3 Once cooled, pour the vinegar liquid over the sliced tomatoes in the jar and put the lid on.
4 Leave until cooled to room temperature, then refrigerate. The pickled tomatoes will be ready to eat the next day and will keep for up to 1 month.
5 Preheat the oven to 130°C (265°F/Gas ½). Season your pork belly with salt and rub with the lemon thyme and garlic.
6 Put the pork belly into a roasting tin deep enough for the pork not to protrude above the lip. Add 150 ml (5 fl oz) of water, cover with baking paper and foil, and cook for about 6 hours, until the meat is tender enough to pull off the rib bones. Check every 2 hours and add a little water if it looks dry. When the pork is done, remove from the oven and set aside to cool, saving the juices.
7 To make the mustard mayo, blitz the eggs and egg yolk with the mustard. Start pouring in the oil, drop by drop, until the mixture begins to emulsify and thicken. Mix in a little wholegrain mustard, to taste, and season with cider vinegar, salt and pepper.
8 When the pork belly is cool enough to handle, cut it into 8 mm (½ in) slices. Heat a pan over medium to high heat. Fry the pork slices on both sides until nicely browned and then brush with some of the reserved roasting juices.
9 Warm the buns through in the oven and slice. Add a slice of pork on the bottom bun, followed by a generous spoonful of the mustard mayo, the lettuce and the pickled green tomatoes. Sprinkle the shallots over the tomatoes, then top with the other half of your bun.

Isaac McHale runs Michelin-starred The Clove Club in Shoreditch, London. You can find me here on a night off sitting at the bar, drinking the city's best Old Fashioneds, snacking on their infamous pine-fried chicken and their smoked cod's roe with rye crackers. Isaac is a total badass chef and his partners, Johnny and Daniel, are complete dudes — they know how to bring massive vibes and provide incredible service in a casual way. I asked Isaac to work on a recipe for this book and he came up with this. 'This sounds like your kinda thing, doesn't it?' And hells yeah, it does. You can get flare fat for this recipe from a good butcher. Isaac says, 'Order flare fat from best-quality rare-breed pigs. There's no point making this recipe unless you have good pigs to start with.'

Smoked Whipped Lardo with Pickled Scotch Bonnets

by Isaac McHale, Owner & Head Chef of The Clove Club

2 kg (4 lb 6 oz) flare fat, minced (ask your butcher to mince it)
cherrywood or oakwood, for smoking
sea salt, to taste
4 sourdough slices, toasted, to serve
maple syrup, to serve
75 g (2½ oz) toasted sunflower seeds, to serve

For the pickled scotch bonnets:
200 ml (7 fl oz) white wine vinegar
2 teaspoons sea salt
50 g (2 oz/¼ cup) granulated (raw) sugar
2 red scotch bonnet chillies, halved and deseeded
2 yellow scotch bonnet chillies, halved and deseeded
2 orange scotch bonnet chillies, halved and deseeded

Makes enough for 4

1 First, make the pickled chillies. Bring the vinegar, salt, sugar and 200 ml (7 fl oz) of water to the boil in a large saucepan.
2 Put the chillies in a clean jar and pour over the hot vinegar liquid, making sure all the chillies are well covered. Put the lid on and allow to cool to room temperature.
3 Line a sieve with muslin or cheesecloth.
4 Put the fat in a shallow bowl and keep cold.
5 Set up your stovetop smoker. Place a piece of foil at the bottom of a large pot big enough to fit the bowl of fat. Add pieces of woodchips and another layer of foil. Heat up your smoker. Dip the base of your chilled bowl of fat in cold water then place into the smoker. Cover with a lid, sealing with extra foil to prevent the smoke from escaping, and allow the fat to gently melt and smoke for 5 minutes.
6 When it reaches 140°C (275°F) (use an instant-read thermometer), switch off the heat. A little crackling will start to float to the surface. Skim this off and reserve for later. Drain the rest of the fat in your muslin-covered sieve into a bowl.
7 Set aside at room temperature for 1 hour. Fill a clean sink with water and plenty of ice. Plunge the bowl of smoked fat in the ice-cold water, whisking continuously. The fat will begin to thicken like whipped cream. Add a few pinches of salt to taste.
8 Chop the pickled chillies into small pieces, add them to the whipped lardo with a bit of the pickling juice.
9 To serve, put a good spoonful of the whipped lardo on top of the sourdough toast, top with sunflower seeds and the reserved bits of crackling, if you like, then drizzle over the maple syrup.

Don't let the presence of the blue corn tortillas make you think this is some holier-than-thou authentic Mexican recipe – it's totally not. But it's got all the flavour components. The blue corn, the smoky braised pork and those zingy, pink onion pickles are just yum. If you can't find blue masa harina flour, substitute with normal masa harina flour or just buy ready-made soft corn tortillas.

Chipotle Pork Tacos with Yucatán Pickles

olive oil
1 large onion, roughly chopped
450 g (1 lb) boneless pork
*   shoulder, cut into chunks*
4 tinned chipotle chillies
*   in adobo sauce, chopped*
2 garlic cloves, crushed
400 g (14 oz) tinned tomatoes
2 fresh oregano sprigs,
*   finely chopped*
200 ml (7 fl oz) beer
1 tablespoon honey
your favourite salsa, to serve
Yucatán Pickles (see page 39)
lime wedges, to serve

for the blue tortillas:
225 g (8 oz/1½ cups)
*   blue masa harina flour*
*   (buy online or at Whole*
*   Foods)*
sea salt, to taste

Makes enough for 4–6

1   Heat a good glug of olive oil in a large, heavy-based pan over medium-low heat and cook the onions for 10 minutes, until soft.
2   Add the pork, chipotle chillies, garlic, tomatoes, oregano, beer and honey.
3   Turn the heat down to low and cook for 3–4 hours, stirring every now and then.
4   Make the tortillas. Combine the masa harina flour with 250 ml (8½ fl oz) of hot water and a good pinch of salt.
5   Knead the dough until it has a Play-Doh-like consistency. If it needs more water, add a tiny bit more. If it's too wet, add a bit more flour. Once you're happy with it, form into a ball, cover with plastic wrap and let it rest for 30 minutes.
6   Divide the dough into golf-ball sized portions. Place each ball in between parchment paper (this will help make them easier to remove once rolled out).
7   Use a tortilla press or rolling pin to create round tortillas.
8   Preheat a heavy-based pan (cast-iron is best) over medium-high heat. Add the tortilla, one at a time, and cook for 20 seconds, until puffed up. Flip over and cook for another 5–10 seconds. Remove and set aside while you cook the remaining tortillas. Keep the tortillas covered with a tea towel to keep them warm.
9   To serve, put a spoonful of the pork on your warm tortilla, top with the salsa and Yucatán pickles and squeeze over some lime juice.

Magnus Reid knows how to do cafe culture properly. Good coffee, eggs, awesome sandwiches, served in a casual, laid-back environment. He's run the kitchens of some of my fave cafes in London, such as The Hackney Pearl, Tuckshop and now, C.R.E.A.M, which happens to be a collaboration with Protein, the creative agency I worked at for four years before going into the world of food. If Magnus is not at his cafe, he's out at some farm picking plums, foraging for wild nettles or doing pop-ups at a friend's hotel or wine bar. He told me he made this dish for a pop-up dinner at this wicked little wine-shop-cum-bar called P. Franco, which I missed, so I asked him to give me the recipe.

Raw Veal with Pickled Grapes
by Magnus Reid, Owner & Head Chef of C.R.E.A.M

for the pickled grapes:
bunch of grapes (I use a mixture of red and green)
500 ml (17 fl oz) good-quality red wine vinegar
4 tablespoons caster (superfine) sugar

for the crispy shallots:
3 shallots, diced
sunflower oil, for shallow frying

for the veal:
200 g (7 oz) free-range veal fillet (organic if possible)
2–4 anchovies, chopped
small handful of chervil, plus extra to garnish (feel free to use another herb, if you don't like chervil), chopped
1 shallot, finely diced
decent glug of good-quality olive oil

Makes enough for 2

1 Slice your grapes in half lengthways. Combine the vinegar and 125 ml (4 fl oz) of water in a pan and set over low heat. When the liquid starts to simmer, add the sugar and stir through for about 5 minutes, until dissolved. Allow the liquid to come to the boil then remove from the heat. Pour into a clean jar or bowl and set aside to cool slightly, until tepid.

2 Add the grapes to the liquid and make sure they are all fully submerged (you might want to put a plate on top of the grapes to push them down into the liquid). Set aside for at least 3 hours, or a few days, to pickle.

3 Next, make the crispy shallots. Dry the diced shallots by pressing down on them with a clean tea towel. Heat the oil in a pan over medium heat. Add the shallots and fry, stirring, for about 15 minutes, until golden brown. It's important to watch them – you don't want them to burn as it will spoil the flavour. Remove using a slotted spoon, and drain on some paper towel. Set aside.

4 Take the veal out of the fridge and use a sharp knife to slice away any larger pieces of fat and sinew. Dice the veal as finely as you like, about 5 mm (¼ in) into cubes. It looks nice when you have even, uniform pieces. Set aside to come to room temperature.

5 Blitz the anchovies, chervil and shallots with the olive oil in a blender or a mortar and pestle.

6 Finally, add this shallot dressing to the veal, a little at a time, and taste as you go. Season the veal when you do this, until you are happy with how it tastes.

7 Form a neat pile, or set the veal in a ring mould, on the plate. Layer the pickled grapes on top, shaking off excess brine as you go. Top this all off with the crispy shallots.

8 Garnish with more chervil, because green stuff is always pretty on a plate.

My friend Gabe Pryce, owner and executive chef of Rita's, makes food that's totally my kinda vibe. He's been bastardising and mashing up various food cultures for years. He calls his food 'Modern American' comfort food, meaning that it takes inspiration from all over the place: Southern American, Jewish, Mexican and Italian. Think peanut brittle, fish tacos, patty melt, *elotes* (Mexican street corn), panzanella and fried chicken with waffles. When Rita's first opened its doors, I supplied their pickles and kimchi. Every week I'd send a taxi with a couple of massive jars their way. It felt like a no-brainer to ask him for a recipe to include in the book. Just like my friend Missy Flynn, also of Rita's, Gabe loves to bring a Mexican vibe to the table – here in the shape of a shrimp tostada. Gabe says, 'This recipe is pretty much a Mexican *smørrebrød*. Which isn't a thing, but I like the sound of it. It's not a traditional Mexican dish at all, but it has shrimp, beans, tequila and beer in it, which in many cultures are traditionally delicious.'

Pickled Shrimp Tostadas with Salsa Borracha

by Gabriel Pryce, Owner & Executive Chef of Rita's

2½ tablespoons sea salt
500 g (1 lb 2 oz) small shell-on shrimp
1 litre (34 fl oz) good-quality wine vinegar (chardonnay, champagne or muscatel)
1 tablespoon granulated (raw) sugar
2 jalapeños
5 bay leaves
2 tablespoons black peppercorns
1 red onion, finely sliced
pared zest of 1 lemon
150 ml (5 fl oz) rapeseed oil, for frying
4 large corn tortillas
2 white onions, finely diced
fresh coriander (cilantro), to serve
sea salt and freshly ground black pepper
soured cream, thinned with a little water
few lime wedges, to serve

1 A day before you want to eat this, pickle the shrimp. Bring a pan of water to the boil with half a tablespoon of salt and add the shrimp. Cook for 2–3 minutes, then drain and plunge into a bowl of ice-cold water. Drain again, then simply slice down the length of the back of the shrimp and remove the poop sack. I'd leave the heads on as they're full of flavour. But you might want to remove the heads, peel and devein, leaving the tails on if you want a bit of a crunch. Place in a bowl and refrigerate while you make the pickling liquid.

2 In a pan, combine the vinegar, remaining salt, sugar and 400 ml (13 fl oz) of water. Bring to the boil and stir until the salt and sugar have dissolved. Remove from the heat and allow to cool to room temperature.

3 Decant the liquid into a clean, airtight container or a large, clean jar. Add the jalapeños, bay leaves, black peppercorns, red onion and lemon zest to the bowl with the shrimp and give it all a good muddle. Pack it all into the container or jar. Pour over the pickling liquid and close the lid tightly. Chill for at least 12 hours or, ideally, overnight, removing from the fridge a couple hours before serving.

4 To make the salsa, preheat the oven to 180°C (350°F/ Gas 4). Drain the chipotle chilli and put in a large roasting tin with the tomatoes, red chillies, onion and beer. Drizzle with loads of olive oil and season with salt. Roast for about 1 hour, until the chilli and tomato skins start to blacken and blister.

recipe continues on the next page

for the salsa borracha:
1 dried chipotle chilli, soaked
in hot water for 20 minutes,
until soft
5 ripe tomatoes
3 red chillies
1 onion, sliced
120 ml (4 fl oz) beer
olive oil
sea salt
1 aubergine (eggplant)
juice of 3 limes
2 shots tequila

for the beans:
2 × 400 g (14 oz)
tinned pinto beans
rapeseed oil
1 small white onion, sliced
3 garlic cloves, peeled
and sliced
1 red chilli, sliced
1 tablespoon chopped
fresh oregano

Makes enough for 4

5   While the tomatoes are roasting, smoke the aubergine. Put the aubergine directly over the flame of a gas hob and char, using tongs to turn every so often, until the skin blackens and blisters on all sides. This will take about 15 minutes. Take off the heat and chop off the stalk and discard. Set aside to cool briefly.

6   When the tomatoes are done, tip them into a food processor and add the aubergine. Blitz to a smooth paste and season with salt, lime juice and tequila. Set aside.

7   Next, make the beans. Rinse and drain the tins of beans, and set aside keeping each tin separate. Heat a glug of the oil in a large frying pan, add the onion, garlic, chilli and oregano and cook over medium heat for about 10 minutes, until the onions are softened and starting to brown. Throw in one tin of beans and cook over medium heat for 5 minutes. Transfer to a blender or food processor and purée until smooth. Remove from blender and stir the remaining whole beans through.

8   Now, heat a pan with the oil and, taking one corn tortilla at a time, fry it quickly until stiff and crispy and a little bit golden brown. Remove the tortilla and drain on some paper towels to absorb any excess oil.

9   Working quickly, spread a tablespoon of the bean mixture across the tortilla in an even and smooth layer, top with the pickled shrimp and the salsa borracha. Garnish the tostada with chopped coriander, finely diced onion and season with salt and pepper. Finish with a drizzle of soured cream and serve with a squeeze of lime.

Everyone has a favourite taco. Mine is a fish taco. To be more specific, the fish tacos from a super-simple shack down the motorway in LA called Best Fish Tacos in Ensenada. In my opinion, they make the very best fish tacos ever – not to mention their huge buffet of salsas and toppings so you can add your own faves. A baja fish taco, in short, is fish fried in batter, served in soft corn tortillas and topped with slaw and some sort of creamy white sauce like a mayo. I like spicing up the slaw with pickled jalapeños and its brine, which creates a zingy and spicy slaw. It's deceptively simple, but it works, so why mess around with it?

Baja Fish Tacos with Pickled Jalapeño Slaw

200 g (7 oz) firm white fish (such as cod), cut into strips
sea salt
150 g (5 oz/1 cup) plain (all-purpose) flour, plus extra to dust the fish
1 medium egg
80 ml (2½ fl oz/⅓ cup) beer (lager)
freshly ground black pepper
vegetable oil, for deep-frying
4 tablespoons DIY Sriracha (see page 86)
4 tablespoons mayonnaise
4 soft corn tortillas
4 wedges of lime, to serve

for the pickled jalapeños:
250 ml (8½ fl oz/1 cup) white wine vinegar
220 g (8 oz/1 cup) granulated (raw) sugar
¼ teaspoon salt
10 jalapeños, sliced
1 garlic clove, peeled and thinly sliced

for the jalapeño slaw:
5 tablespoons pickled jalapeños (above), plus 2 tablespoons of the brine
½ head white cabbage
large bunch of coriander (cilantro), finely chopped
sea salt, to taste

Makes enough for 2–4

1 To make the pickled jalapeños, heat the vinegar in a pan over a medium to high heat, and add the sugar and salt. Whisk until dissolved.
2 Put the sliced jalapeños and garlic in a clean jar. Remove the pickling liquid from the heat and carefully pour over the jalapeños and garlic.
3 Put the lid on and allow to come to room temperature. Put the jar in the fridge. Your pickle will be ready to eat after 2–3 days.
4 Make the slaw. Put the pickled jalapeños in the food processor and give them a quick blitz. Transfer to a bowl.
5 Finely slice the cabbage using a mandoline or simply use a sharp knife. Put the cabbage in the bowl with the jalapeños.
6 Stir in the brine and coriander, then leave for 2 hours. Taste for seasoning and add more brine if needed.
7 Put the fish in a bowl and season with salt.
8 In a separate bowl, whisk together the flour, egg and beer to make the batter.
9 Put the extra flour in a shallow bowl or on a plate. Lightly dredge the fish in flour and shake off any excess.
10 Heat the oil to 190°C (375°F). When the oil is hot, dip the fish in the batter, and carefully add to the hot oil. Fry for about 3 minutes, until golden. Remove the fish using a slotted spoon and drain on paper towels.
11 Combine the DIY Sriracha and mayo together in a bowl.
12 Heat the tortillas in a dry skillet or pan until they bubble up slightly. Keep warm on a plate under a damp towel.
13 To serve, spoon the slaw onto the tortillas, top with the fish and drizzle over the sriracha mayo. Serve with a squeeze of lime.

This recipe is inspired by my heroine Christina Tosi, who runs Milk Bar in New York City. A sister brand to Momofuku, Milk Bar is a bakery that makes incredible cookies (I ask any friend who visits NYC to smuggle me back at least three of their corn cookies), does the most insane soft-serve ice cream (yuzu cherry, anyone?) and oh yeah, they TM'd Cereal Milk. This one time, at Milk Bar, I ordered a croissant that was made by folding kimchi butter into the dough rather than normal butter, with blue cheese as a filling. It was a revelation. When Christina's first book *Momofuku Milk Bar* was published, the recipe for this was included and I tried to make them. I failed. It's really, really hard to make croissants!

So I came up with the idea to turn it into a sandwich, which is a lot easier. I've been selling these grilled cheese sandwiches at market stalls and pop-ups for years and people love them. It's so racy! It's crazy! It shouldn't work! You can't put kimchi in sandwiches! Yes you can. And it's delicious. I use Neal's Yard Dairy for cheese, because it's the best.

Kimchi & Stilton Grilled Sandwich

softened butter, for spreading
4 slices of good-quality
* white bread*
3 tablespoons F.A.T Sesame
* Kimchi (see page 71)*
2 tablespoons finely chopped
* spring onions (scallions)*
2 tablespoons good-quality
* Stilton, or other similar*
* blue cheese, crumbled*
2 good handfuls of good-
* quality, grated Cheddar*
small handful of cheese curds
* (optional)*

Makes 2 sandwiches

1 Spread the butter on one side of each slice of bread, and don't be shy. If using a toastie maker, put 2 slices of bread, butter side facing down, on to the grill.

2 If you don't have a toastie maker, heat a large, heavy-based pan over medium heat. Put 2 slices of bread, butter side facing down, in the pan.

3 Now add the toppings in this order: kimchi, spring onions, Stilton, Cheddar, and if you like, cheese curds. Top the sandwiches with your remaining slices of bread, butter side facing up.

4 If using a toastie maker, press down hard so things don't start falling out, and toast until done. If using a pan, put a sheet of foil or baking paper on top of the sandwiches followed by a casserole dish (the weight of the casserole will press the sandwich down). Fry over medium to low heat, until golden on one side, then flip over and repeat with the other side. When ready, the cheese should be melted and the toast golden brown.

DRINKS

I'm all for big, complex flavours with my food, but weirdly I've never been a huge fan of complicated drinks or cocktails. I'm more of a wine and beer kinda gal. Of course, there are the classics that everyone loves, including moi.

A proper homemade ginger beer, a dirty Martini, a good Bloody Mary – these are some of my absolute go-tos from retox to detox.

Duke's Hotel Bar in London's Mayfair is known to serve the best martini in London – some even say it's the best in the world. It's rumoured that Ian Fleming got the inspiration for his 'shaken not stirred' line for Bond in here. If you're ever in London or in the area and you've not been, please go. Just don't have more than just one martini – these bad boys are incredibly strong. I like them dirty, with a bit of olive brine. Here, I use dill pickle brine instead of olive.

Pickletini

½ teaspoon dry vermouth
ice cubes
250 ml (8½ fl oz) vodka
2 tablespoons Cucumber Dill
   Pickle juice, chilled (see
   page 17)
dill pickle, to garnish

Makes enough for 2

1 Pour the vermouth into a cocktail shaker and add the ice cubes.
2 Cover and shake for a few seconds, then strain into chilled martini glasses.
3 Now pour the vodka and pickle juice into the cocktail shaker.
4 Cover and shake for half a minute, then strain into the chilled martini glass. Garnish with a dill pickle.

Whether you love bloody Mary as a hangover cure or as part of a decadent brunch spread, it's a great classic cocktail that everyone seems to have their own favourite version of. This is mine. It's spicy, boozy, sweet and savoury, and I honestly don't think there are many things out there that don't benefit from a bit of kimchi.

Kimchi Bloody Mary

1 tablespoon F.A.T Sesame Kimchi (see page 71)
500 ml (17 fl oz) tomato juice
2 tablespoons DIY Sriracha (see page 86)
1 tablespoon Worcestershire sauce
1 tablespoon cider vinegar
1 tablespoon gochugaru (Korean chilli powder), plus extra to serve
sea salt and freshly ground black pepper
lime wedge, to serve
ice cubes, to serve
125 ml (4 fl oz) vodka
celery stalk, to garnish
pickled chillis, to garnish

Makes enough for 2

1 Blitz the F.A.T Sesame Kimchi, tomato juice, DIY Sriracha, Worcestershire sauce, vinegar and gochugaru in a food processor until smooth.
2 Season with salt and pepper to taste (this will depend on the strength of your kimchi; if it's already quite salty you might not need to add more salt).
3 You've now made your Bloody Mary base mixture. You can either put this through a fine mesh strainer and discard the pulp to get a very smooth juice, or you can leave it a bit chunky, which I personally prefer.
4 Use the lime wedge to rub the rim of two glass tumblers and dip the rims in salt and gochugaru.
5 Serve over ice and vodka with a stick of celery and a pickled chilli.

Keep it simple or go all out on the garnish! Things like pickled okra, celery, chillies, shrimp, or shiso leaves work pretty well.

Kawaii! These super-cute things may look like miniature watermelons but, in fact, they taste of cucumber and lime! Cucamelons are a central American delicacy, can be found all over Mexico, and are also known as 'mouse melon' or 'Mexican sour gherkin'. They lend themselves perfectly to pickling.

Cucamelon Cornichons

100 g (3½ oz) cucamelons
1 garlic clove, peeled
3 tarragon sprigs
60 ml (2 fl oz) elderflower
  vinegar (you can also use
  white wine)
60 ml (2 fl oz) cider vinegar
1 tablespoon sea salt
pinch of black peppercorns
pinch of yellow mustard seeds
½ bay leaf

Makes 1 × 300 ml (10 fl oz) jar

1 Rinse the cucamelons and, while doing this, pick off the blossom ends with your fingers and discard. Place the cucamelons in a clean jar.
2 Slice the garlic into thin slivers and add them to the jar. Top with the tarragon sprigs.
3 Combine the vinegars, 125 ml (4 fl oz) of water, salt, peppercorns, mustard seeds and bay leaf in a pan and bring to a boil.
4 Remove from the heat and immediately pour the hot vinegar-brine over the cucamelons into the jar. Leave to cool completey, then refrigerate. These are ready to eat after 3 days and will keep for up to 2 weeks in the fridge.

There's the story of the pickleback originating in Philadelphia, and then there's the Brooklyn one – where Reggie Cunningham from Bushwick Country Club bar in Brooklyn, NYC, was storing pickles for McClure's when the pickling company first started up. Story is that a girl asked for a shot of the juice alongside her whiskey. Reggie drank a couple, it cured both his cold and hangover, and a new drink was born. How it works: you shoot a shot of whiskey, and you chase it with a shot of brine. The pickle brine works magically to neutralise the burn of the alcohol.

Pickleback

1 shot good-quality whiskey
Cucamelon Cornichon
  (see above), to garnish
1 shot pickle juice of choice,
  strained

Makes enough for 1

1 Garnish your shot glass with a Cucamelon Cornichon.
2 Shoot the whiskey, chase it with the pickle juice.

I came across water kefir not very long ago at my friend Dougie's Brighton-based restaurant, Silo. They make pretty much everything in-house: their 'espresso mushrooms' are grown from the coffee grounds from the restaurant (and are incredibly delicious) and they mill their own flour on site. Their basement is a collaborative project with Old Tree Brewery, where they make their own beer, cider and delicious fermented soft drinks, such as water kefir, ginger beer and kombucha. It's sustainability taken to the next level. I drank their sea buckthorne water kefir and I was sold immediately. It's a yummy, fermented soft drink and it's good for your gut, and I'm all for things that taste nice and are good for you!

Rhubarb & Jasmine Water Kefir

2 jasmine tea bags
160 g (5½ oz/1 cup) granulated (raw) sugar
2 rhubarb stalks, sliced into 2 cm (¾ in) chunks
4 tablespoons raisins
1 slice lemon
2 tablespoons water kefir grains

Makes 1 litre (34 fl oz) jar

1 Brew the tea in a large, clean jar with 1 litre (34 fl oz) of boiling water. Add the sugar and stir to dissolve. Leave to cool completely.
2 Add the rhubarb, raisins, lemon and water kefir grains.
3 Cover the jar with muslin (cheesecloth) and secure with butcher's string. You don't want to close the jar with a lid as you need to let out the rising carbon dioxide. Leave it in a warm place for 24 hours.
4 Give the kefir a taste. The longer you leave it, the more sour and bitter it will get. After 2–3 days you can strain it and remove the fruit and spices. Store in the fridge for up to 1 week.

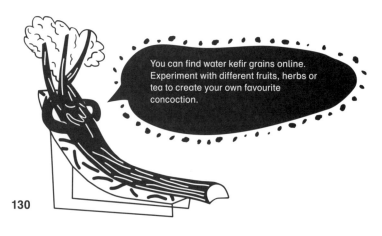

You can find water kefir grains online. Experiment with different fruits, herbs or tea to create your own favourite concoction.

Homemade ginger beer is wonderfully refreshing on a warm day, or you can, of course, mix it with your favourite whiskey brand. It's easy to make, it just takes a bit of time, two weeks to be exact. Leave it on your kitchen countertop so you can keep an eye on it and watch it fizz and bubble. On day three you should start to see some bubbles. If you ever see a layer of ginger sitting on top, stir it. You want to mix in some air as fermented foods and drinks thrive in aerobic conditions.

Ginger Beer

14 teaspoons grated fresh ginger (2 teaspoons a day for 7 days)
14 teaspoons granulated (raw) sugar (2 teaspoons a day for 7 days)
4 litres (7 pints) mineral or filtered water
juice of 2 lemons

Makes 2 × 2 litre (3½ pint) bottles

1 Pour 375 ml (12½ fl oz) of water into a clean wide-mouth jar and add 2 teaspoons of grated ginger and 2 teaspoons of sugar. Stir well.
2 Cover the jar with muslin (cheesecloth) and secure with butcher's string. Place the jar on your kitchen counter so you can keep an eye on it for the next week (see pic opposite).
3 Each day for the next 6 days, uncover the jar and add 2 teaspoons of sugar and 2 teaspoons of grated ginger to the mix and stir well. Cover the jar again and put it back in its place.
4 After feeding it on day 7, strain the mixture through a muslin-lined sieve into a very large bowl or bucket. You want to try and squeeze out as much liquid as possible. This is your ginger beer starter.
5 Pour the mineral or filtered water into the bowl. Add the ginger beer starter and the lemon juice and stir.
6 Decant the ginger beer into clean plastic bottles and cover with muslin (cheesecloth), secure with butchers string. You don't want to close the bottles with a lid as you need to let out the rising carbon dioxide. Taste the ginger beer after 2–3 days and once you're happy with the flavour and fizz, screw the lids on to the bottles and refrigerate.
7 Store in the fridge for 1 week before drinking.

Missy Flynn is the ultimate #girlboss! She works hard, plays hard, runs her own restaurant, makes killer drinks, oh, and she's a TOTAL hottie. Both she and I are obsessed with everything Mexican, which she channels into some of the best drinks I've ever had, such as this *tepache* – a fermented fruit-rind drink (traditionally pineapple) that has its origins deep in Mexican history. Missy says, 'My first experience of *tepache* was seeing it served in little plastic bags off the side of the road in Mexico. There's not much alcohol in it from the natural fermentation but you can't help feel a little badass walking around in the sun drinking a bag of fermented pineapple funk. It's insanely refreshing and pops up everywhere in Mexico. From *horchata* to *agua de jamaica* and all kinds of fruit *frescas* and *paletas*, I love the way Mexicans turn local fresh fruit, herbs and spices into delicious coolers that taste best when you stumble upon them on street carts.'

Tepache
by Missy Flynn, Bar Boss & Owner of Rita's

1 large ripe pineapple, thoroughly washed, leaves and base removed
approximately 500 g (1 lb 2 oz/2 cups) piloncillo (unrefined cane sugar) or soft light brown sugar
1 dried ancho chilli, toasted
6 whole black peppercorns
1 large cinnamon stick

Makes 1 × 2 litres (3½ pint) jar

1 Prepare your pineapple. Cut away the rind from the flesh and slice the pineapple in half. Remove the core and slice the rind into 2½ cm (1 in) thick strips. Roughly chop the core, and discard/eat the flesh.

2 Place the rinds into a 2 litre (3½ pint) capacity, clean jar with the sugar. The sweetness of this drink depends entirely on taste but using the same weight of sugar as the weight of the pineapple rinds and core works for good balance. Mix these up so the sugar coats all of the pineapple.

3 Add the toasted ancho chilles and 1½ litres (51 fl oz) of filtered water in a pan. Add the peppercorns and cinnamon, and heat gently for about 3–5 minutes to make a lukewarm spiced tea. Do not let it boil.

4 Take off the heat and pour the liquid into the jar, along with the spices. Give it a stir then cover the jar with muslin (cheesecloth). Secure with butcher's string and set aside somewhere warm for 24 hours. The fermentation occurs due to the reaction between the natural yeast and sugar in the fruit and the brown sugar. The time it will take to ferment can vary, but after 24 hours, check the jar and skim off any white froth on the top. Bubbles will tell you if it's come to life!

5 Leave to ferment for a further 12 hours, or until bubbles are more prominently visible on the surface. Over-fermenting will make a bitter vinegar, so at this stage, strain the mixture through a fine sieve, discard the fruit rind and the spices and pour the liquid back into the jar. Reseal and let it sit overnight at room temp.

6 Refrigerate for up to 1 week and serve neat, or use in the recipe for Tepache-ilada (see page 136), or mix 2 parts Tepache with 1 part sparkling water. Serve chilled over ice.

Missy and I served this as part of a Day Of The Dead Party we hosted together in the downstairs Night Elm bar at Rita's a year ago. It's Missy's twist on *michelada*, a spiced *cerveza* (beer), and it's one of her favourite ways to use *tepache*. 'The *tepache* adds depth and sweetness from the pineapple and a spiciness that wakes you up. The beer bubbles party with the pineapple bubbles. If you're smart enough to prepare this in advance, it will see you through a hangover in a flash.' To make a quick and delicious beer cocktail you can prepare *tepache* in advance and store it in the fridge alongside a crate of beer and some fresh limes. You don't need much else.'

Tepache-ilada

by Missy Flynn, Bar Boss & Owner of Rita's

lime wedge, to serve
sea salt
1–2 tablespoons Tepache
  (page 134)
1 tablespoon fresh lime juice
Mexican hot sauce, of choice
  (something slightly sweet
  works best, like Valentina
  or Cholula), to taste
pinch of cracked black pepper
dash of Worcestershire sauce
ice cubes, to serve
Mexican beer, dark or light
  (1 bottle per person)
sliced red chilli, to serve

Makes enough for 1

1 Use the lime wedge to rub the rim of a beer glass, then dip it into the salt.
2 Add the Tepache, lime juice, hot sauce (I like mine hot!), pepper and Worcestershire sauce.
3 Fill the glass with ice, top up with beer, and add chilli and a lime wedge, if you like. Mix, drink, enjoy.

Index

About Freddie Janssen

Pickle-lover Freddie Janssen moved to London from
Maastricht, Holland in 2008. She is the founder of F.A.T,
a pop-up café, supper club and purveyor of pickles, kimchi
and sauces, all made by Freddie, which are stocked in
restaurants and stores across London. She also runs a
market stall at one of the capital's newest food destinations,
Druid Street Market.

Thank Yous

Thanks to everyone that has helped to shape this book and supported my journey from working in advertising to becoming #foodserious.

My mum, dad and sister, who have been crazy supportive over the last few years even though they never really knew what it was that I was doing. But they let me do my thing and always encouraged me to work hard and get shit done.

Alice and Terence, for starting up F.A.T together and being super cool with letting me go on with just F without the A and T.

Henry and Charly, a massive thanks for letting me turn our house into a crazy lab with bottles of pickles and bubbling jars everywhere. I promise the fridge is all yours again now.

Kate and Kajal from Hardie Grant. First of all, thank you for believing in me and for asking me to write a book, and then giving me huge amounts of freedom and letting me go on to make the most awesome-looking book ever.

Which brings me to Milena. You have taken my brief of 'I want it to look like *Cloudy with a Chance of Meatballs 2*' to the next level with your 'pool party' illustration theme. Thank you, thank you, thank you, for the best drawings in the world.

Helen Cathcart, the photographer for this book. Thank you for making pickles look sexy and going way beyond just shooting pickles in Mason jars. You made that shit look awesome!

Claire Warner. Thanks for designing the most kick-ass book. I love it!

Kate Wanwimolruk, my recipe editor, for all the time and effort spent on shaping my text – I really appreciate it.

Suzanne, my dearest and oldest friend from back home. For being super-supportive for the 15 years I've known you, inspiring me to be my best, work hard and stay happy. Love you, dude.

Crane Cookware, thanks for the beautiful pans, they are the best.

James and John. James, for helping me become #foodserious. John, for being the best boss-man ever, and for letting me take far too many days off work to write this thing.

Taahir. For helping me not sound stupid :-)

And thanks to everyone that contributed recipes – Missy Flynn, Gabriel Pryce, James Lowe, Magnus Reid and Isaac McHale.

 by Freddie Janssen

First published in 2016 by Hardie Grant Books

Hardie Grant Books (UK)
52–54 Southwark Street
London SE1 1UN
hardiegrant.co.uk

Hardie Grant Books (Australia)
Ground Floor, Building 1
658 Church Street
Melbourne, VIC 3121
hardiegrant.com.au

British Library Cataloguing-in-Publication Data. A catalogue record
for this book is available from the British Library.

ISBN: 978-1-78488-033-0

Publisher: Kate Pollard
Senior Editor: Kajal Mistry
Editorial Assistant: Hannah Roberts
Cover and Internal Design: Claire Warner Studio
Illustrator © Melina Bucholz
Photography © Helen Cathcart
Photography Assistant: River Thompson
Prop Stylist: Linda Berlin
Copy editor: Kate Wanwimolruk
Proofreader: Charlotte Coleman-Smith
Indexer: Cathy Heath
Colour Reproduction by p2d
Author picture on page 142 © Issy Croker
Picture on page 120 © Victor Frankowski
Printed and bound in China by 1010

10 9 8 7 6 5 4 3 2